YOUR 30-DAY JOURNEY
— T·O —
Being a

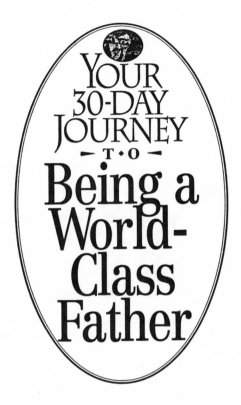

YOUR 30-DAY JOURNEY — T·O — Being a World-Class Father

C. W. NEAL

OLIVER NELSON

THOMAS NELSON PUBLISHERS
Nashville

Published in Nashville, Tennessee, by Oliver-Nelson Books, a division of Thomas Nelson, Inc., Publishers, and distributed in Canada by Lawson Falle, Ltd., Cambridge, Ontario.

The Bible version used in this publication is THE NEW KING JAMES VERSION. Copyright © 1979, 1980, 1982, Thomas Nelson, Inc., Publishers.

Printed in the United States of America.

Library of Congress Cataloging-in-Publication Data

Neal, C. W. (Connie W.), 1958–
    Your 30-day journey to being a world-class father / C. W. Neal.
        p.   cm.
    ISBN 0-8407-9626-9 (pbk.)
    1. Fatherhood—United States.   2. Fathers—United States.
3. Father and child—United States.   I. Title.   II. Title: Your
thirty-day journey to being a world-class father.
HQ756.N43   1992
306.874'2—dc20   92-7717
                                                              CIP

1 2 3 4 5 6 — 97 96 95 94 93 92

Contents

•

Introduction

Being a world-class father is not something that happens by accident. Can you think of any worthwhile position, relationship, or accomplishment that is achieved and maintained without focused attention and effort? Can you imagine any business growing and flourishing under the leadership of someone who had never considered what was entailed in making the business succeed? Obviously not. Neither can you become a world-class father without having a clear vision of what that means, setting definite goals, mapping out a plan of action, and applying yourself to the task. The same principles that are customary in making businesses grow and thrive can be exercised as you build into your children's lives and futures.

No man wants to feel inadequate as a father, and yet most men worry, to some extent, whether they are on the right track. You may wonder how you measure up, without ever having thought through exactly what standard of fathering you are trying to meet. Perhaps the fact that men's roles are quickly changing in our society makes it more of a challenge to know what is expected of fathers. At work, the roles and expectations are clear-cut. If you're doing a good job, you know it, and the sense of satisfaction can be immediate. That same sense of satisfaction can be had by fathers who have clearly defined for themselves what it means to be the best father they can be. This journey is designed to take you through the process of clarifying for yourself what it means to be a world-class father, then lead the way as you take decisive action in that direction.

This 30-day journey is based on the belief that any father has the ability to be a world-class father. Some men have the advantage of being raised by a father who gave them emotional sustenance and strong leadership, which may predispose them to being a world-class father. Other men may have the disadvantage of being raised without a father or having a father who was emotionally absent or abusive. Although the journey may be easier for some than others, every father has the potential to become a fully competent, loving, and effective father. You can be a world-class father if you are willing to apply yourself to the process.

What Is a World-Class Father?

What is a world-class father? There was a time when most people in our society would have answered that question in similar terms. In days gone by, a man knew what was expected of him and what was not. Previously, our culture defined a world-class father primarily in terms of being a good financial provider, protector, and disciplinarian. This is not true in today's world. In a majority of families the father is no longer the sole provider, nor is he considered exempt from aspects of parenting that had been relegated to the mother just a generation ago. Even if today's father could live up to a positive role model provided by his father, the role he saw being modeled might be obsolete! It's no longer enough to "bring home the bacon." Perhaps it never was.

The burgeoning men's movement in this country echoes the cries of a generation of men. They say the image of the father whose peak responsibility was to provide, protect, and discipline wasn't enough. They speak of father-hunger and grieve the years they lived under the roof dad provided so well without feeling his love they needed so deeply.

The reevaluation of a father's role in this generation can protect you from assuming a role that doesn't really meet your children's needs. The lack of societal definition offers you freedom to experience a full and satisfying relationship with your children.

My idea of a world-class father is depicted in the three spheres of this diagram:

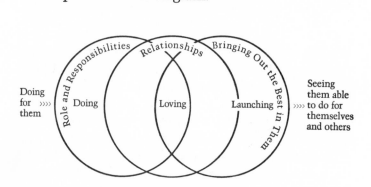

A world-class father has a positive balance in these three areas of fathering: the doing (performance), the loving (building relationship), and the launching (bringing out the best in them). You have certain responsibilities as a father in terms of providing for the needs of your children and doing for them until they are able to do for themselves. In addition, the children need your love and a positive relationship with you. The children also need your help in growing up, developing into competent adults, and being prepared to face life successfully.

In the context of this journey you will be seeing yourself in these three primary areas: (1) revitalizing your performance of your fathering role, (2) strengthening your relationship with each child, and (3) motivating your children to bring out the best in them. To do any of these well to the exclusion of the others results in problems.

PERSONAL EVALUATION

- Have you felt the influence of the changing societal roles and changing expectations of fathers?
- Have you experienced what could be described as a fathering identity crisis as you tried to figure out what your role is supposed to be?

ACTION

Make a fathering notebook by adding a section to an organizer you already use or using a three-ring binder. Copy the diagram of the three areas that make up a world-class father into your notebook. Write a brief definition of what you think it means to be a world-class father, centering on these three areas.

Write a detailed description of each of your children, including what you know of their personalities, physical traits, intellects, and so on. Seal these in an envelope and put them away until Day 30.

REFLECTION

As you consider the three elements of fathering in the diagram:

- Which area needs the most work?
- In which area do you feel most confident?

ENCOURAGEMENT

The fact that you are taking this journey shows that you genuinely care about being the best father you can be. Your effort combined with your concern will bring about positive results.

FOOD FOR THOUGHT

What is a world-class father supposed to be? Consider this quote:

> Children want to feel instinctively that their father is behind them as solid as a mountain, but, like a mountain, is something to look up to.
> —Dorothy Thompson
> *Ladies' Home Journal*
> June 1956

The Commitment to the Journey

Every journey requires energy to get you from here to there, accurate directions to make sure energy isn't wasted going the wrong way, and a commitment to take each step and keep going until you reach the destination. Take a look at each element to see if you are ready for the journey.

Energy

Most men don't prepare for fathering in any formal sense. Children come along, and many fathers assume they should know how to be a world-class father without applying the energy it takes to gain an education or skills for the job. Certainly, natural love for your children and common sense applied to situations that arise will carry you so far. However, to be world-class at anything requires focused energy to develop natural abilities. What talented athletes or salesmen would reach the heights of their respective professions without expending a tremendous amount of energy to gain further education and practice skills that lift them above the level of mediocrity? This is just as true in the personal arena as it is in the professional one—and ultimately much more important!

Directions

Accepting directions will make your journey easier. Comedians make light of an experience common to many men. They tell of a husband and wife driving around hopelessly lost, and yet the husband would rather die than stop to ask someone for directions. Chuckles from the men in the audience show that there is some truth to the charge. You may feel uncomfortable asking for directions relating to being a world-class father. If you have never taken this journey before or if the landscape has changed since you last considered fatherhood, you would be wise to accept directions from others. Helpful directions are available from a host of sources. Even as you accept directions, you are still in the driver's seat. You determine where you are, how far you are away from your destination, and what roads you need to travel to get there.

Commitment

You can achieve anything if you are willing to make a commitment to it and follow through with whatever steps are necessary. The choice is yours to make. The first commitment you are being asked to make is to devote at least thirty minutes each day for the next 30 days to the completion of this journey. There is also the personal commitment of courageously facing some issues that may be uncomfortable and challenging as you examine and reflect on being a world-class father.

PERSONAL EVALUATION

- Are you willing to expend the energy it will take for this journey?
- If you don't have much energy left for this journey, where does it go?
- In what areas of your life have you expended energy to learn and gain the skills needed to excel? Do you really consider these endeavors to be more valuable than fathering your children?
- Are you willing to accept directions for the journey?
- Are you willing to make the necessary commitments?

ACTION

My Personal Commitment

I, _____, am serious about my desire to be a world-class father to *(list the names of your children here)* _____
_____.

I am willing to invest at least thirty minutes a day, from each of the next 30 days, to focus on this journey. I will plan to take this time each *(circle one)* morning, lunchtime, afternoon, or evening.

I understand that to reach this goal, I must be willing to grow on a personal level, to exercise courage to look at myself honestly, and to endeavor to meet any challenges. I will do *my* best in all of these areas.

Since my goal is to be a world-class father, not a

perfect father, in the next 30 days, I will not focus my attention on how far I fall short of the ideal. I will focus my attention on *moving forward* from where I am today toward what I want to be.

I make this commitment to myself this _____ day of _____ , 19_____.

_____
Signature

Set aside a section of your fathering notebook to compile reflections.

REFLECTION

What feelings were evoked as you considered embarking on your journey to being a world-class father?

ENCOURAGEMENT

Your willingness to systematically work through this journey demonstrates that you value your fathering role and relationships. You and your children will benefit from your commitment and the things you will discover during your journey.

FOOD FOR THOUGHT

One person with a commitment is worth one hundred who only have an interest.

—Mary Crowley

A Man with a Mission

Most successful organizations have a mission statement that sums up the purpose for which the organization exists. The mission statement captures the dream and crystallizes it into a tangible reality that members can keep in mind. A clear mission statement allows everyone involved in the organization to understand the ultimate goal and to see how each fits into the overall picture. When someone is off track, the effective leader is able to use the mission statement as a marker to help the individual understand where the behavior departs from accomplishing the purpose of the whole.

What is the mission of your family? You may never have thought in these terms before. By crystallizing your family mission into a clear statement, you establish the purpose and values that keep everyone connected and on track.

PERSONAL EVALUATION

What do you desire most of all for your family? Allow yourself to see your life from another perspective. Imagine that you can look back on your family from a time fifty years in the future. What would you want to see result from growing up in your family?

What dreams for your family would you want to see realized?

As you imagine yourself looking back on life in your family as you hope it can be, answer these questions: What have your children learned and understood about life, love, God, relationships, family, and friendships? How has their knowledge of world history, geography, mathematics, language, sports, science, arts, and literature been encouraged and expanded? What has happened in your personal development as the result of being their father? How have you achieved your best, developed your talents, preserved your health, and so on? How has your life been affected by responsibly fulfilling your role as father and sharing the gift of yourself with your children?

Can you imagine being able to heal the wounds in your life, breaking destructive family patterns that were passed down to you, escaping cycles of bondage to addiction and compulsive behavior, overcoming any debris of abuse in your own life or the lives of your children?

ACTION

Allow these thoughts to prompt your hopes and dreams for your family. Write and complete each statement in your notebook:

- At the end, when I was looking back on my life, I would see . . .
- My children would grow up to be *(character qualities rather than occupation)* . . .

- My children would come to me and say . . .
- My children would overcome . . .
- My children would develop these attitudes to face life successfully . . .
- My children would regard themselves . . .
- Financially, my children would . . .
- My children would be spared . . .
- In eternity I would see them . . .

Clarify your dreams for your family into a brief mission statement. Reduce your statement to one or two sentences that each family member can memorize. Write this mission statement in your notebook.

REFLECTION

Were you able to hope for the future without hesitation? Was it easy or difficult to define what your family is all about? Why do you think that was the case?

ENCOURAGEMENT

Your willingness to clarify your thinking will help every member of your family grow together and stay on track.

FOOD FOR THOUGHT

A man whose life mission does not incorporate the well-being of his children and family may lose at life even while accomplishing the mission he set out to achieve.

Who's in Charge Here?

You can be a confident leader of your family. Leadership is not some mystical quality imbued in the lives of men who seem to be natural leaders. To exercise leadership you need to understand the purpose of your family, establish common goals, clarify principles that will govern behavior, and then take decisive action toward the fulfillment of your shared purpose and individual goals. You have already begun to develop your leadership skills by determining your family mission statement. You will continue to develop and apply leadership skills as you complete your 30-day journey.

Having a father who is willing to take charge in leading the family is a benefit to each member. If all members of your family are to function well and achieve their best in life, you need to commit yourself to exercising leadership within the family. When you function fully in a father's leadership role, you provide security and confidence for your children.

When a father's authority is exercised fairly, there are many benefits: children know precisely what is expected of them, those under authority are relieved of the burden of responsibility being carried by others, and each child can focus on doing his or her part well (which should be in keeping with individual ability and level of understanding) without having to be concerned with the whole operation. As children learn to respect and respond to authority, they are better prepared to participate successfully in society. They learn how to function well under authority and also how to exercise authority over others.

As a father and leader, you are in a position to affirm the value of your children, display respect for them, and release them to excel at life as they learn to function within the authority structure of the family.

The best leaders deeply respect the value and abilities of each person. Leaders are required to make decisions that will not please everyone yet work for the good of all in achieving common objectives. The choices they make will shape and limit the options available for those under their leadership. Leaders learn to delegate, follow up on the progress of those they lead, and encourage individual excellence. Leaders also must be accountable and held responsible for their actions. And they must be willing to make sacrifices for the ultimate good of those they lead.

Certain biblical guidelines set standards for responsible leadership:

> Husbands, love your wives, just as Christ also loved the church and gave Himself for her. . . . So husbands ought to love their own wives as their own bodies; he who loves his wife loves himself. For no one ever hated his own flesh, but nourishes and cherishes it, just as the Lord does the church (Eph. 5:25, 28–29).

And you, fathers, do not provoke your children to wrath, but bring them up in the training and admonition of the Lord (Eph. 6:4).

Abuse will not take place in the family where the man at the top displays this kind of love to accompany his authority.

PERSONAL EVALUATION

- Are you clearly designated as the head of your family?
- Do you respect and support your wife's position of authority over the children and require their submission to her?
- Are you and your wife in agreement regarding the authority structure of the family?
- Have you ever been accused of abusing your authority?
- How well do you comply with what God requires of you? Do you display self-sacrificial love to your wife consistently? Are you bringing your children up without exasperating them and provoking their wrath?

ACTION

In your notebook draw an organizational chart that shows lines of authority and who is in submission to whom as they are currently being lived out within your family. Then draw an organizational chart showing how the family authority should be run with you at the head.

Hold a family meeting to clearly explain your position of authority within the family and how your leadership will benefit everyone. Make sure all of them understand their position and what it requires of them in relationship to the others above and below them in the authority structure.

REFLECTION

Have members of your family ever been the victims of the abuse of authority?

Where might any fear, anger, and other uncomfortable emotions originate when discussing family authority?

How can you be sensitive to these issues and still take your place as the head of your home?

ENCOURAGEMENT

Leadership can be learned. By taking the time to study and consider your leadership role, you can learn to be a world-class father.

FOOD FOR THOUGHT

You do not lead by hitting people over the head—that's assault not leadership.
> —Dwight D. Eisenhower

Teamwork: Defining Roles and Responsibilities

Every child has basic needs that parents are responsible to meet. With the changes in our society, role expectations over who is responsible to care for particular needs have become confused. The father may assume something to be the mother's responsibility only to find that she doesn't see it the same way. This type of confusion or disagreement can hurt your children. Parents must work as a team to care for the needs of their children, even when the parents are no longer married.

Today you will be considering the needs of your children. A world-class father takes responsibility to see that his children's needs are responsibly covered. You may not do all of these things yourself, just as the CEO of a corporation doesn't do everything himself. However, the father's role of leadership requires making sure the needs are met, and if no one else will take responsibility, it falls to you.

PERSONAL EVALUATION

As you read this list of parental responsibilities, rate yourself on a scale of one to ten for how well you think you make sure each responsibility is carried out. (One is poor; five is adequate; ten is excellent.) Put a star next to any that you have previously never considered your responsibility or assumed belonged to the children's mother alone.

PROTECTION   RATING
1. Provide a safe environment . . . .
2. Teach safety rules . . . .
3. Personally supervise children . . . .
4. Provide trustworthy caregiver when away . . . .
5. Protect from other siblings . . . .
6. Teach self-protection skills . . . .
7. Provide preventive medical/dental care . . . .
8. Protect innocence/sexual boundaries . . . .

PHYSICAL NEEDS   RATING
1. Furnish a healthy and balanced diet . . . .
2. Provide appropriate clothing . . . .
3. Provide medical care as needed . . . .
4. Provide dental care as needed . . . .
5. Provide appropriate level of privacy for sexual
   development and a healthy acceptance of gender . . . . .
6. Provide and enforce necessary amounts of rest (sleep
   and quiet times while awake) . . . .

EDUCATION   RATING
1. Provide opportunity for education . . . .
2. Teach values at home . . . .
3. Answer questions and explain things . . . .
4. Provide a place for learning and study . . . .
5. Help them learn study skills . . . .
6. Supply tools for learning . . . .
7. Read to them and provide age-appropriate reading
   materials . . . .
8. Affirm their potential and progress . . . .

9. Provide extracurricular learning experiences ....
10. Recognize, encourage, and affirm strengths and talents

SOCIAL SKILLS   *RATING*

1. Provide social opportunities ....
2. Teach manners and social skills ....
3. Give correction in a nonshaming way, helping them feel confident in social settings ....
4. Allow and encourage participation in age-appropriate groups and organizations ....
5. Allow, monitor, and encourage age-appropriate friendships ....

PERSONAL HYGIENE   *RATING*

1. Provide a clean environment ....
2. Teach them at an appropriate age about personal cleanliness ....
3. Make sure hair is groomed ....
4. Check that clothing is clean, in good repair, and appropriate size ....
5. Teach them how to keep their living space reasonably clean and orderly ....

VALUES   *RATING*

1. Share personal values at their level ....
2. Provide value-related feedback to the media ....
3. Teach problem solving ....
4. Teach right from wrong ....
5. Set clearly defined limits and expectations for behavior
6. Give consistent discipline and correction ....
7. Maintain family traditions ....
8. Practice the values espoused ....
9. Admit mistakes and allow them to learn from your life ..
10. Explain values in the context of religious beliefs ......

SPIRITUAL NOURISHMENT   *RATING*

1. Provide elements of beauty in life ....
2. Pray for them and with them ....
3. Encourage hopes and dreams ....

4. Provide positive religious experiences . . . .
5. Read them Bible stories, stories that have moral
   lessons, etc. . . . .
6. Celebrate holy days in an uplifting and educational way
7. Allow and encourage them to wonder and to seek
   understanding of life . . . .
8. Allow them to voice doubts and wrestle with beliefs in
   order to develop a personal faith . . . .
9. Affirm their rights as human beings to feel, think,
   perceive, interpret, want, choose, and imagine . . . .

ACTION

Circle any areas where you need to be more effective. You will use them later in the journey as the bases of your goals. Sit down with your children's mother, and discuss each item. Negotiate until each item is accepted as a commitment by at least one parent. If the item is something the children need individually from both father and mother, discuss whether each of you is willing to accept this responsibility.

REFLECTION

Were there areas of responsibility that you had never considered before? How do you feel about accepting the responsibility that comes from being the head of your home?

ENCOURAGEMENT

By considering your children's needs, you are a step closer to making sure those needs are met, which is what a world-class father does.

FOOD FOR THOUGHT

To be sure, working—that is, earning a living—is one aspect of fathering. It's one means that the father has of extending protection to the family. But it's just one. If he concentrates on this to the exclusion of other aspects it becomes not a form of fathering, but an escape.

—Myron Brenton
The American Male

Evaluating Relationships with Your Children

For many men, building relationships with their children may be the most challenging facet of being a world-class father. You may find it more difficult to evaluate relationships than responsibilities since responsibilities are within your control and relationships involve another human being, which takes some control away from you. It may help to consider this an adventure, which can yield wonderful discoveries within your children and your own heart.

Each child is a unique person; therefore, you need to evaluate your relationship with each child separately. Your relationships will be different because of many factors: the child's age and sex, shared or differing interests, the season of your life when each was conceived, circumstances, health, and the number and ages of other children in the family.

Each relationship involves two people. You will be looking at how well you contribute to the relationship from your side. All children have a hunger for the love of their father. They will respond positively to your love if it is communicated consistently.

PERSONAL EVALUATION

Rate yourself on a scale of one to ten for how well you do in the following areas in your relationship with each child. (One is poor; ten is excellent.)

EMOTIONAL NOURISHMENT   *RATING*
1. Listen to the child . . . .
2. Validate feelings . . . .
3. Display physical affection . . . .
4. Maintain eye contact while talking . . . .
5. Verbally express love . . . .
6. Verbally express praise and appreciation of achievements . . . .
7. Offer encouragement . . . .
8. Give special attention . . . .
9. Attend special events . . . .

FUN TIMES   *RATING*
1. Play games together . . . .
2. Go enjoyable places together . . . .
3. Have unstructured time together . . . .
4. Do what the child enjoys . . . .
5. Listen to music and/or sing . . . .
6. Participate in sports or outdoor games . . . .
7. Enjoy toys . . . .
8. Read to or with the child . . . .
9. Create things together . . . .

THE CHILD AS AN INDIVIDUAL   *RATING*
1. Recognize talents and strengths . . . .
2. Recognize areas of weakness . . . .
3. Know close friends . . . .
4. Know school friends . . . .
5. Know fears . . . .
6. Know worries . . . .

7. Know favorite things (entertainers, food, books, color, subject of study, clothes, etc.) ....

8. Know hopes and dreams ....

9. Understand temperament ....

10. Know signs of when rest is needed ....

MY ATTITUDE TOWARD THE CHILD   *RATING*

1. Accept the child as he or she is ....

2. Affirm right to feel as he or she does ....

3. Affirm right to develop own ideas ....

4. Affirm gender (I like that you are a boy or girl) ....

5. Affirm growing ability to care for self ....

6. Display and affirm unconditional love (apart from approval or disapproval of behavior) ....

7. Affirm healthy desires ....

8. Treat with respect ....

9. Practice the golden rule with the child ....

10. Support the child in ventures to learn and grow ....

11. Am fair and consistent ....

12. Show kindness ....

EXPECTATIONS   *RATING*

1. Confident that my expectations are in keeping with age level ....

2. Clearly express my expectations and listen to make sure child understands those expectations ....

3. Confident that my expectations are compatible with other healthy demands on the child's life (school, other parent's expectations, job, etc.) ....

4. Confident that my expectations are within the child's ability to perform ....

ACTION

Create a summary of areas that need attention in your relationship with each child. Select one area to strengthen in your relationship with each child. Write these out in the form of a commitment.

REFLECTION

After you've rated yourself on your relationship with each child, keep your reflections on this topic confidential. Each child must feel loved and appreciated fully. Children may misinterpret differences in these relationships to mean that you love one more than another.

Take some time today to reflect on your relationship with each child and any theories you may have about why some relationships are stronger than others.

ENCOURAGEMENT

By giving your attention to strengthening your relationships with your children, you are showing yourself and them respect.

FOOD FOR THOUGHT

No man can possibly know what life means, what the world means, what anything means, until he has a child and loves it. And then the whole universe changes and nothing will ever again seem exactly as it seemed before.

    —Lafcadio Hearn
      Lafcadio Hearn: Life and Letters, Vol. 2
      edited by Elizabeth Bisland

Defining Family Policy

The *New American Webster Dictionary* defines *policy* as "a course of conduct based on principle or advisability." *Principle* is defined as "a fundamental truth or doctrine on which others are based." Your principles and beliefs shape your expectations of your children's conduct. However, many fathers haven't taken the time to consider and communicate their principles or to define family policy for their children.

In a work setting, most employees are given an employee handbook or a policy and procedure manual when hired. It tells them precisely what conduct is acceptable and why compliance to certain standards of behavior is important within the company. The manual defines the consequences for disregarding or disobeying policy, warning and probation procedures, how to file complaints, company benefits, and so on. Everyone goes by the book. Whenever a question arises about appropriate conduct, the employees can look first to the policy spelled out in specific terms to see if there is a prescribed code of conduct for the situation. If there is not, they can look to the principles used to guide company policy to help them make a wise decision in keeping with the spirit of the company. When everyone adheres to company policy, employees don't have to worry and wonder if

25

they are pleasing their supervisor or fall prey to the whims of someone in a bad mood. The well-written manual frees employees to securely function in their position so that they can perform and grow continually in keeping with the mission of the organization.

You can give your family this sense of security and freedom to grow by defining family policy for them. Communicating family policy will let your children know exactly what is expected of them and why, along with the consequences they can expect if they disregard or disobey the code of conduct family principles prescribe. Writing out family policy will allow you to clarify your thinking, plan to discipline in a way that will best train and correct your children, and have a framework for developing policy for new issues. It also gives your children an arena for discussing issues of real importance and for negotiating more independence as they grow up. When you have family policy based on principle in a form children can grasp from an early age, they can use it as a model for learning to make their own decisions in life.

PERSONAL EVALUATION

This exercise will allow you to evaluate foundational principles for family life. Listed are principles basic to every family in general terms. You may not agree precisely with the principle as stated. If you disagree, change the statement to reflect your principles. Your goal in this exercise is to get the feel of evaluating your principles and the family policy emanating from those principles. Try to think of other principles you hold that influence what you expect of your children.

Principle	*Policy*
We, as your parents, will always love you, no matter what happens.	When you are in trouble, you can come to us for help.
Honesty is basic to family relationships.	Dishonesty in any form will have serious consequences.
	You are expected to tell the truth, the whole truth, and nothing but the truth.
Respect for each other is essential, as is respect for authority.	Respect is shown by caring for personal property, privacy, the feelings of others, and so on.
	Disrespect is shown by *actions*, such as . . . ; *tone of voice*, such as . . . ; *nonverbal cues*, such as . . . ; *saying things*, such as . . .

Parents are responsible to correct and discipline their children. Appropriate correction proceeds from love.

Correction will occur whenever you are doing something that
(1) is dangerous,
(2) you know to be wrong,
(3) defiantly violates our principles.

ACTION

Designate a section of your notebook as your family policy and procedure section. Make up a standard form as follows, leaving space for your comments. Duplicate as many as you need.

Principle: Here is what we believe about _____.
Policy: Here is what is expected of your conduct __

_____.
Benefits: This is important because _____.
Consequences for misbehavior: Here is what will happen if you don't conduct yourself in this way

_____.

Put your family policy into writing for as many issues for which you already have clear expectations of conduct. Some topics you may consider are home care, financial responsibility, jobs, mealtimes, homework, visiting away from home, entertainment options, complaints/grievances, dating, showing disrespect to parents, fighting, and so on.

REFLECTION

Does your family operate on double standards, expecting your children to do as you say, not as you do? If that is the case, do you feel disqualified from establishing a standard of conduct for your children? Did you have a clear code of conduct in your family when you were a child? How did the presence or absence of such policy influence your feelings about this exercise?

ENCOURAGEMENT

By taking the time to clearly define and communicate your expectations, you are giving your children security and reducing the amount of conflict within your home.

FOOD FOR THOUGHT

Children cannot be made good by making them happy, but they can be made happy by making them good.

—E. J. Kiefer

Training and Discipline

The great boxer Joe Frazier was quoted in the January 1972 *Reader's Digest* as saying:

> You can map out a fight plan or a life plan, but when the action starts, it may not go the way you planned, and you're down to your reflexes—which means your training. That's where your roadwork shows. If you cheated on that in the dark of the mornin', well, you're gettin' found out now under the bright lights.

Your children need training to be able to win the fights they will face in life, and you're responsible to train them. The training must start when they are young; it must be consistent and disciplined. If you train them well and require consistent discipline, you will be able to let them go into the ring of life with confidence that they can hold their own. If you slack off or neglect discipline, there will be a price to pay. When the fight comes at adolescence and they're out there in the ring on their own, you may have to watch them take a beating.

Training and discipline depend on knowing what you are trying to train into their lives. You have to know your goal before you can discipline them in that direction. Each child will have a bent, a unique approach to life, so your method of training should be adapted to fit the temperament, personality, and level of understanding of each child. Knowing your family policy and knowing your children individually give you an excellent basis for being able to give them the training and discipline they need to be prepared for life.

In the years between becoming members of your family and starting out on their own, your children need to gain confidence and skills to become productive members of society. They need to know about practical matters and also the spiritual realm. In the Bible, God commands parents to pass down their knowledge of Him.

You must convey to your children your values and faith in God. It is not enough to assume they will make their own choices regarding religious values, anymore than it would be to assume that they are capable as children of making their own choices about other important decisions. In fact, since the spiritual realm is intangible, you must make it come alive for them. They will develop their own values in time, but you must give them a foundation to build on.

How are you supposed to do that? The answer is, a little at a time. According to Jim Burns, a trainer of youth workers, all successful training endeavors involve four phases: (1) I do it for you; (2) I do it and you watch; (3) You do it and I watch; and (4) You do it and I do something else. For each child, you can identify certain tasks at any of the given phases of training. For example:

TAYLOR (age two)

- I do it for you: Making meals.
- I do it and you watch: Putting on shoes and socks.
- You do it and I watch: Putting away small toys.
- You do it and I do something else: "Building" with blocks.

CASEY (age six)

- I do it for you: Driving to school.
- I do it and you watch: Using the computer.
- You do it and I watch: Reading a book.
- You do it and I do something else: Taking a bath.

The ideal is to train them to be as self-sufficient and as confident in their own abilities as possible at each stage of development. When they are not able to meet their needs, you should make sure those needs are met. As they become more capable, you should train them to make wise decisions and develop skills to take care of themselves. If you continue to do for them what you should be teaching them to do for themselves, you do them a great injustice. They will not be equipped to face life.

PERSONAL EVALUATION

Consider the tasks on the following list. Use a number to designate where you think each age group should be in the launching process for that particular task.

Skill	Infant	Preschool	Six to Twelve	Teen	Young Adult
Feeding	1	2–3	3	4	4
Dressing					
Dental hygiene					
Brushing hair					
Bathing					
Washing hair					
Choosing clothes					
Cooking					
Handling finances					
School decisions					
Choosing friends					
Choosing foods					
Use of time					
Hobbies to pursue					
Education choices					
Religious education					
Dating choices					
Determining bedtime					
Getting a job					

1 = I do it for you.
2 = I do it and you watch.
3 = You do it and I watch.
4 = You do it and I do something else.

ACTION

Circle any areas on this list where you feel your children need more in-depth training at this point in their lives.

List what you want to train into your children before they leave the nest. Include the following: things you want them to know how to do; values; domestic skills; coping skills; knowledge; marriage and relationships; faith in God; other.

REFLECTION

Consider this proverb: "Correct your son, and he will give you rest; yes, he will give delight to your soul" (Prov. 29:17). How do you feel about the responsibility of training and correcting your children? What can you see as consequences for neglecting training and discipline of your children? In what areas do you rely on someone else to make sure your children are trained and disciplined?

ENCOURAGEMENT

When you train, correct, and discipline your children in a consistent way, you are displaying your true love for them and your concern for their ultimate well-being.

FOOD FOR THOUGHT

Doting parents would do well to remember that in doing everything for a child and expecting nothing we do the child a disservice. Children as a rule do not want to be indulged; they want to be responsible. Overindulgence is the ultimate insult, for when you "spoil" a child you are practically saying, "I know you aren't capable of being civilized and considerate and contributing and I won't expect it of you."

—Hannah Lees

To Know Them Is to Love Them

Anne Frank and her family were forced into hiding during the Nazi holocaust when Anne was entering puberty. In the dark, cramped quarters of their hiding place, Anne recorded her reflections on life. When the family was captured, to perish in the holocaust, Anne's diary was preserved and published under the title *Anne Frank: The Diary of a Young Girl*. Certainly, the diary revealed the stark horror of living in the midst of fear and hatred. It also revealed a glimpse of what may secretly be hidden in the heart of every young girl and boy. Although Anne and her father were trapped together in a tiny room, I wonder if he knew the longing of his little girl's heart. I wonder if her father would have been surprised at this entry: "I'm not jealous of Margot [her sister], never have been. I don't envy her good looks or beauty. It is only that I long for Daddy's real love: not only as his child, but for me—Anne, myself."

Your children long for your real love: not only as your children but for themselves, for the unique individuals God created them to be. They long for you to notice what is special about them, to care about what is of interest to them, to know them as individuals distinct from their brothers and sisters.

You are in a position to strongly influence how your children come to understand their inherent value. One basic theory of sociology is that people see themselves the way they believe the most important person in their lives sees them. The way they think you, as their father, see them (or don't see them) has the power to create or destroy self-esteem, the power to inspire greatness and encourage accomplishment. What your children *perceive* as your view of them will go a long way toward shaping the basis of how they see themselves.

PERSONAL EVALUATION

Consider each child in the following ways:

Age and Developmental Stage

What are the special needs of a child this age?

Sexuality

Does this child have a healthy understanding of sexuality appropriate for his or her age? Do I have open lines of communication with him or her regarding sexual issues?

Personality and Relationship

Do I see him or her as an introvert or an extrovert? Do I accept the child, or do I try to change the personality to be something I prefer? Do our personalities seem to generally mesh easily?

Learning Style

Which of these four learning styles best describes what I have observed about this child?

1. *Innovative (feeling)*—learns from specific experiences; relates to people easily; likes to share ideas.
2. *Analytic (watching and listening)*—observes carefully before making a judgment; views things from different perspectives; seeks facts.
3. *Common Sense (thinking)*—logically analyzes ideas; plans systematically; acts upon intellectual understanding of situation.
4. *Dynamic (doing)*—gets things done; takes risks; prefers trial-and-error method.

Physical Health

General health is excellent, good, fair, or poor. Does a physical limitation or health problem limit the ability to enjoy life as other children?

Talents and Special Abilities

What are the areas of apparent talent: music, art, mechanical abilities, drama, computers, poetry, creative writing, debate, athletics? What special skills and abilities has the child developed by following interests?

Education and Intellectual Abilities

The intelligence level is *(circle one)* genius, above average, average, below average, developmentally disabled in some way. What subjects does the child enjoy learning about? What are favorite books?

Interests and Hobbies

How is free time spent? What are the child's hobbies, favorite TV shows, favorite musical artists, and favorite sports? What does the child want to be when he or she grows up?

Social Skills

Does the child know how to interact well with others of the same age? Does the child know how to resolve differences? Does the child understand and practice socially acceptable behavior and manners?

Interaction Within the Family

How does the child get along with siblings? Are there open lines of communication: with father? with mother?

Spiritual Development

How extensive are the child's spiritual interests? Does the child have a personal faith in God? Does the child want to attend religious functions?

Areas of Brokenness

Has the child experienced any kind of physical, medical, or accidental trauma that had an apparent emotional effect? Has the child been separated from one or both parents for any length of time? Has the child lost someone close through death or a move? Has the child been victimized or abused in any way? If these areas of brokenness exist, what has been done to help the child recover?

ACTION

Based on the exercise you've just completed, write out a description of each child in your notebook. Go beyond a surface description to try to capture the heart and personality as well. Focus on the good in each one. You are not to be critical of what you would like them to be or do differently. Share these descriptions with someone who knows the children well. Ask the person to give you feedback on how well you know each one; listen to insights you may have missed about your children. Seal these written descriptions in an envelope and keep with the descriptions you wrote on Day 1. You will open these on Day 30.

REFLECTION

Do you feel that your parents genuinely know you for who you are? How does it feel to be known, understood, and appreciated or to be misunderstood, neglected, or rejected by a parent? What value do you see in knowing and appreciating each child individually?

ENCOURAGEMENT

By taking the time and attention required to know and appreciate each of your children, you are giving them what their hearts secretly long for.

FOOD FOR THOUGHT

It is a wise father that knows his own child.
—Anonymous

Fathering by Objectives

Today you will clearly define your objectives related to being a world-class father. All you have to do is to look back over the exercises you have already completed and choose what you are willing to take action on at this point in your life. You will draw your goals and objectives from the evaluations you've already made. You will select a few goals to focus on initially during the remainder of your journey. As you successfully achieve them, you can replace them with new goals.

Remember, we defined a world-class father as having a positive balance in these three areas: the doing, the loving, and the launching. So, you will be setting goals in three primary areas: (1) revitalizing your performance of your fathering role, (2) strengthening your relationship with each child, and (3) motivating your children to bring out the best in them.

Being world-class doesn't mean being perfect. Everyone has room for improvement, and you can't do everything at once; therefore, you need to prioritize. Here's a tip to decide what to work on first. Your love for each child and your good relationship embrace the other two facets of fathering. Focusing on having the love strongly in place and clearly communicated allows room for error and time to work on the other two areas.

You will choose specific objectives to achieve within the remainder of your journey. The short-term objectives will take you in the direction of your long-term goals. As you begin to achieve objectives in each facet of fathering and to keep a balance in these three areas, you will be well on your way to being a world-class father.

PERSONAL EVALUATION

Step One

Go back to "Day 5: Teamwork: Defining Roles and Responsibilities." Pick one area in which you wanted to be more effective and highlight it.

Step Two

Go back to "Day 6: Evaluating Relationships with Your Children." Pick one area in which you wanted to strengthen your relationship with each child and highlight it. You may have the same area of interest for all of your children or a different objective for each child.

Step Three

Look back at Day 9 and the information you have written about the unique qualities for each of your children. Pick one area for each child where you would like to take action to bring out the best you see in him or her. You could affirm a positive quality or help develop a talent.

Step Four

Write out a clear and specific description of each goal so that you will be able to tell if you have achieved your objective at Day 30. You may want to define the immediate and long-term versions of the same goal.

Let's use a relationship-strengthening goal as an example. In my relationship with Marnie (age fifteen), I will make a point of spending more time with her when we can talk without the distraction of the other children. I will create opportunities when she can talk freely (inviting her to go with me anywhere that I am planning to go on my own, taking a snack to her in her room in the evening, driving her whenever she needs a ride somewhere). I will listen to her concerns, her ideas, and her feelings. I will make a point of trying to understand her perspective. I will know that I have reached this goal when I consistently am able to reflect back to her what she has related to me and have her confirm that I am understanding her fully.

ACTION

Create three new sections in your notebook: "Being More Effective in My Performance of Fathering Roles and Responsibilities"; "Strengthening My Relationships with My Children"; and "Motivating: Bringing Out the Best in Them." Place the written goals you've selected in the appropriate category.

Make a form with these headings across the top— "Dreams," "Goals," "Tasks," "People Involved," "Timing," and "Checkup"—and photocopy several of them. Now that your thinking is clarified in terms of a few specific goals, you will take the information from your evaluations and written goals, then slot it into these forms.

- In the "Dream" column, write down the long-term result that your objective will lead you toward.
- In the "Goals" column, write down the specific measurable result you are trying to achieve. Ask yourself, How will I know when I achieve this goal?
- In the "Tasks" column, write down all the tasks involved.
- In the "People Involved" column, write down who is responsible for each task or who you need to cooperate with to complete the task.
- In the "Timing" column, write down the date you plan to complete each task and the overall goal; take note of who else has to accommodate a schedule for you to be able to complete each task and reach your goal in the time required.
- In the "Checkup" column, write the date you are checking to see how you are doing and how near you are to completing the task and reaching the goal.

REFLECTION

What are the benefits you see from having specified goals and objectives for being a world-class father? What frustrations are you experiencing in the process of evaluating the various elements of fathering?

ENCOURAGEMENT

By conducting an analysis of your fathering, setting goals, creating a plan of action, and following up on your progress, you are going to get the results you seek. You will be a world-class father. You also show that your family is as important as the other areas of life where you apply yourself to setting specific goals.

FOOD FOR THOUGHT

Winning at the workplace is a shallow triumph if you're losing at home. Those who can maintain a healthy bottom line in both environments are achieving the greatest victory of all.

—Victor Kiam
Living to Win

How Will the Objectives Be Met?

Once you have determined precisely what you want to focus on in your journey to be a world-class father, you need to plan strategies that will allow you to integrate those goals into your everyday life. Here are some key ways to meet the objectives you have chosen for yourself.

Availability

An Italian proverb says, "Absence is the enemy of love." Your presence with your children is the best strategy for expressing your love and setting the stage for everything else you hope to accomplish in fathering. You may feel like you are in a bind. Perhaps, you would like to spend more time with them but don't have any uncommitted time. One solution to this dilemma is to integrate your children into your routine whenever you can. You don't have to do something special every time you are with them. Chances are that they are interested in having time with you, regardless of what else is going on. You could probably include them when you are running errands, cleaning out the garage, shopping, washing the car, grooming, driving somewhere, participating in your favorite hobby, and so on.

These shared moments will give your children familiarity with you on a day-to-day basis, which tells them you are available whenever they need you. As this becomes a regular part of your father-child relationship, your children will likely turn to you with their needs more often.

Accessibility

Many successful organizations operate an open-door policy with their employees. Employees are taught that if they ever have a concern, problem, question, or need, they are welcome to bring that issue before management. When this policy is practiced consistently, employees learn that they are genuinely welcome to turn to their leaders for guidance and help.

This same principle carries over to your relationship with your children. In *An English Year*, Nan Fairbrother said, "There are so many disciplines in being a parent besides the obvious ones like getting up in the night and putting up with the noise during the day. And almost the hardest of all is learning to be a well of affection and not a fountain, to show them we love them, not when we feel like it, but when they do." One key to practicing an open-door policy with your children is to make sure you welcome them whenever they venture out to seek your help. All children need to know that if they have a need, their father is a well of affection for them to draw from.

Younger children also need parents to be a fountain, issuing advice and guidance continually. As they grow older, especially when they reach adolescence and are sorting life out for themselves, they need the "spouting" to stop. Adolescence is the time to turn off the fountain, to listen, and to allow them to draw from you as they discover their own needs and problems. You acquire tremendous power to influence them at this juncture by becoming that well they can draw from whenever life leaves them thirsty: for answers, affection, guidance, support, correction, and so on.

Delegation

You do not need to personally attend to every facet of your child's life. However, you are responsible to make sure that all the bases are covered in keeping with your family values. Our society is rapidly changing. School and governmental programs are taking over more and more of what was once the domain of parental influence. Issues of significance dare not be left in the hands of those outside your family, who may not share your values. Consciously choose what can and cannot be delegated to others.

Consistency

Children need consistency in terms of what they can expect from life. Once you have clarified your family mission, values, and policy, you have a foundation for ensuring consistency. You can let your children know precisely what your family stands for, what you want for them, what is expected of them, and what they can expect from you.

PERSONAL EVALUATION

- Are you in the habit of including one of your children as you go about your routine tasks?
- Do you have an open-door policy with your children? If so, do they often come to you with their concerns, problems, and needs?
- Would you characterize yourself more as a fountain (spouting out what you want them to take in) or a well (available for them to draw from)? Is this appropriate for their ages?
- Do you think you delegate enough, too much, or too little regarding the raising of your children?
- Do you find that it is relatively easy or difficult to maintain consistency with your children?

ACTION

Decide if you want to include your children in your daily routine tasks. If you do, invite or include one of your children with you today during a time when you would have normally been by yourself.

Decide if you want to have an open-door policy for your children. If you have not already clearly communicated your open-door policy, do so.

In your notebook list all the things you can think of related to raising your children that are delegated to others. Next to each item, note *Y* or *N* for whether you really want someone else taking over that responsibility. Brainstorm ideas for how you can effect changes to take back responsibility for those things you don't want delegated to others. Make another list of everything you do directly for your children that might be safely delegated to others so that you can be freed up to take care of those issues you consider to be of the utmost importance.

REFLECTION

Consider what you are doing positively in each of these areas. What positive effects do you see from the degree to which you already practice being available, accessible, responsible to delegate, and consistent with your children?

ENCOURAGEMENT

Your time and effort spent in planning how to best accomplish your fathering goals will make being a world-class father easier than you may have thought.

FOOD FOR THOUGHT

The thing I was always warned against about waiting a long time to have children was that I wouldn't be able to throw a ball with them. Well, I'm here to say that I don't think it's going to be a problem. Either I'll throw balls with the best of them and that'll be that, or I won't and it won't matter. . . . Two plus years into this fatherhood business, I know at least that what kids require of their father is a lot of attention, a lot of love and, I suspect, if mine ever reach the age of understanding, a lot of that too. They can find other people to throw balls at them.
—Carey Winfrey
as quoted in *Papa, My Father*
by Leo Buscaglia

Periodic Reviews and Revisions

A primary benefit of clearly evaluating and defining life as a father is that you are in a better position to improve and learn as you go along. When pursuing a mission or goal, you always need to receive feedback and to make revisions along the way. Consider sports teams, corporate executive boards, military leaders, and so on. Those who are successful have built periodic reviews and revisions into their way of life. These reviews usually take the form of regular meetings to keep the members of the organization in touch with one another, to allow for input from all members, to solve problems, to come up with new ideas for reaching common goals, to give correction to those who are off track, and to lend support to one another.

Many families struggle to stay connected, given the host of options vying for everyone's attention. The family meeting can provide a format that will serve many good purposes.

Here are some suggested topics to include in regular family meetings:

- Upcoming schedule for the month and how schedules conflict or coincide
- Time for members to tell what they are involved in currently and how the family could lend support

- Discussing problems and possible solutions
- Discussing important issues that may affect the family (considering a move, vacation plans, finances, and so on)
- Resolving conflicts between family members
- Instruction from parents
- Sharing something that made each one happy, proud, or sad
- Commenting on something each one appreciated in another family member that week

As the head of the family, you will be able to use these meetings to teach, to listen to your children's input, to hear complaints, to resolve conflicts, to coordinate plans, to correct wrong conduct, to clarify misunderstandings, to affirm your children, to demonstrate unity with your wife, and to highlight areas of family policy that merit attention at the time.

You will also be able to see where you may be getting off track yourself and make revisions in your conduct. For example, during the discussion of what each one is involved with and what is needed from others in the family, you may hear a recurrent theme that your children and wife need more of your time or attention. This feedback becomes a form of checks and balances, helping you consider whether you are overcommitted outside your family. You have the opportunity to reevaluate your commitments and draw back from some of them or to explain to your family the special circumstances that demand your attention away from home.

The effective meeting has the following elements: consistency, some fun (perhaps special refreshments), time for each person to contribute and be heard, a summary of what was discussed and decided, and follow-up from the previous meeting to make sure that what was decided has been complied with.

Family meetings should be held at regular intervals, such as weekly and monthly. In addition, meetings can be held for special purposes, such as responding to a family emergency or preparing for a holiday season. You may want to have an informal agenda to lend credence to the process. Each person can share ownership in the process by taking turns helping with refreshments, being asked for comments, and being held accountable to follow through on a specific task. All family members should be allowed to put any topic that is important to them on the agenda. Someone can be designated to take notes of what is decided and what is to be done by whom.

PERSONAL EVALUATION

How do you currently ensure ongoing two-way communication and cooperation within your family? Have you ever held a well-planned family meeting? If not, what are your reasons for not doing so? Examine each one and ask yourself if the obstacles outweigh the potential good of trying to keep everyone on the same track in this way. Can you think of a better way?

ACTION

Plan and hold a family meeting. Explain to your family that you have been taking this journey and that holding this meeting is your assignment. Your children will probably like the prospect of your having real homework. They may complain, but if you can share your enthusiasm and sell them on the benefits, they may be excited about the idea. Plan the meeting well, so they know what to expect. Keep the meeting brief and each member involved; that way the children won't get bored. The day before the meeting, ask each member individually if there is anything in particular to discuss at the family meeting. Add those topics to your list.

Here is a sample format to follow. You can amend it as you see fit.

Introduction (3 min.)

Present your reasons for the meeting, special topics on the agenda, and rules of conduct.

Rules
1. Everyone will get a chance to talk.
2. Listen when others talk.
3. Don't be afraid to bring up what is important to you. (Let them know that you will make sure no one is disregarded or ridiculed.)

Discuss Schedule for the Week (10 min.)

Discuss what is happening that needs the others' attention (special events, afterschool activities, working late). Is the calendar planned so that members can get where they need to be at the time they need to be there?

What's Going on with You? (10 min.)

Ask each family member to indicate what is going on and ways the rest of the family can help.

How Are You Feeling? (10–20 min.)

Have family members tell one thing that made them feel good (happy, proud, excited), one thing that made them feel uncomfortable (angry, sad, worried, afraid), and one funny thing that happened to them or that they heard during the last week. As the director, keep everyone focused on the person sharing feelings; affirmation of each person is important.

Problems or Complaints? (10–20 min.)

Allow each person to be heard, then facilitate discussion of possible solutions. It's your job to lead the discussion, maintain order, summarize solutions, and give direction.

Appreciation

Encourage each person to name one thing appreciated in the life of another family member that week.

Special Topics

You may or may not have special topics.

Summary

The designated person summarizes the major decisions and identifies who is responsible to take action in the coming week. This step can also include appointing the person to plan refreshments for the next meeting. (Note: Your children will be more highly motivated to participate if the meeting is associated with some small special treat.)

REFLECTION

How did the meeting go? If you were to continue having these meetings on a regular basis, what benefits do you anticipate? What changes would you make for future meetings? What skills do you want to develop to become better able to facilitate this meeting? Are you willing to continue having a family meeting for six weeks to see how it goes? What did you learn that was news to you?

ENCOURAGEMENT

You may not feel completely comfortable holding a family meeting. Nevertheless, your family sees you taking the lead in a tangible way.

FOOD FOR THOUGHT

The art of progress is to preserve order amid change and to preserve change amid order.
—Alfred North Whitehead
Forbes magazine
December 1, 1957

Making the Most of Mistakes

Perfection is not expected of a world-class father. You can have a positive influence on your children even through your mistakes and failures. In his book *Father: The Figure and the Force*, Christopher P. Andersen notes a study that reflects this fact:

> Dr. Bernard Saracheck of the University of Missouri at Kansas City studied the lives of 187 entrepreneurs, many of them legendary business figures like John D. Rockefeller, James Cash Penney, and Henry Ford, and discovered that although most of their fathers were self-employed, none were successful. The fathers' self-reliance strengthened their sons' resolve to pursue independent commercial activity, but equally important was the father's bitter lesson of failure. Knowing how horribly dehumanizing poverty could be, these men vowed that this would never happen to them. The only instances where the son completely rejected Dad as unworthy of emulation occurred not in response to any business failure on Father's part, but only after the father spurned his son because of dislike, disinterest or distrust.

Everyone makes mistakes in business and in personal life. Fathers are allowed room to make mistakes without failing their children. If your mistakes are understood in the context of love, they can be used as lessons your children can grow from. The one thing that is guaranteed not to fail is real love. As long as you love your children, show them that you like them, maintain interest in them, and believe in them, you have room to fail without destroying their lives or losing their affection.

If you pretend to be perfect and demand that your children join in the pretense, they will not be able to turn to you when they fail. Allowing them to see your imperfections and mistakes doesn't have to diminish your stature in their eyes. They are watching to see how you deal with mistakes and failings as a model for how they can deal with theirs.

Just as there are no perfect fathers, there are no perfect children. At times, your children will fail to live up to your expectations, disappoint you, make mistakes, and rebel. It's all part of the nature of being human. When they make mistakes, are you prepared to respond with the kind of love and forgiveness you would hope for if your failings were exposed? The Bible says that love "bears all things, believes all things, hopes all things, endures all things. Love never fails" (1 Cor. 13:7–8). If your love is based on your commitment to love them unconditionally, you will be able to love them even when you disapprove of their behavior. Your children's moments of failure give you the opportunity to show them that you love them regardless of their mistakes.

PERSONAL EVALUATION

- Have you made mistakes you fear will negatively affect your children?

- What lessons have you learned from these mistakes that could be of benefit to your children as they grow up?
- Have you made peace with yourself, God, and others with regard to areas of failure in your life?
- Do you expect perfection of yourself? If you do, are you encouraged to learn that even your perceived failures can turn into success in the lives of your children?
- Do you expect perfection of your children, or do you allow them room to acknowledge and learn from their mistakes?
- Can you display love at a time when your children's behavior calls for disapproval of their actions? Think of a time when you were able to do this.

ACTION

Think of one mistake or failure in your life that your children can learn from. Make it into a story with a lesson that can be communicated in a way appropriate to your children's ages. Tell your children the story. If your children are too young to understand, write the story in your fathering notebook, and plan to share it with them when they are old enough.

REFLECTION

Are you deeply uncomfortable with the thought of your children seeing you as less than perfect? If you are, what do you think has caused you to connect being lovable with having perfect performance?

ENCOURAGEMENT

Once you realize that you need not be perfect to be world-class, you can experience a great sense of relief and hope. If you have the courage to accept your own humanity and that of your children, complete with all the imperfections, you make room for real love and honest vulnerability.

FOOD FOR THOUGHT

Children most need love when they least deserve it.

> I teach my child and I tell other
> children of all ages—
> preschool, in school, in college,
> and out:
> That nothing is done finally and
> right.
> That nothing is known
> positively and completely.
> That the world is theirs, all of it.
> —Lincoln Steffens

Call in the Consultants

One secret of successful leadership is knowing when you need help and being willing to get the best help available. Excellent leaders understand they cannot know everything to make their organizations flourish. They function fully in the areas of their expertise and recognize where they need the input of others with detailed knowledge of a particular topic. They determine what they need to know outside their scope of reference, then they call in the consultants.

In a government, business, or military setting a common practice is to rely on the wisdom of others whenever necessary. If the president of the United States were to fail to recognize situations where expert consultation from advisers was required, the security of the entire country would be endangered. Great leaders aren't expected to know it all; they are expected to be well informed whenever making crucial decisions.

Great fathers aren't expected to know it all either, but they, too, need to be well informed to make the many important decisions regarding their children. However, this understanding doesn't necessarily carry over into the life of the family. Many men seem to believe that they should know how to care for their families without having to ask for help and expert advice. Some men may feel ashamed to reach out for the knowledge and help needed to be a world-class father. This type of thinking can endanger the security of your family. Every father needs the wisdom and contributions of others to keep up with the changing demands of his role. A world-class father is not hesitant to call in the consultants whenever he needs them.

Tremendous resources are available for every imaginable facet of fathering. Once you have identified specific goals and objectives, you can easily find resources to give you knowledge, help you develop skills, and provide practical assistance and support. Here are some ideas about how to track down resources.

Step One

Identify the area where you need help or more information.

Step Two

Check at your local library for books on the topic or related topics. Most libraries have a wide variety of books on parenting and fathering issues. Ask a librarian to recommend books.

Step Three

Contact organizations set up to deal with your area of interest. A great resource for family-related issues is Focus On The Family. You can call them and receive leads about almost any conceivable family issue. The telephone number is 719-531-3400.

Another way to track down groups and organizations is to use your telephone directory. Look under city, county, state, and federal government for numbers of agencies. If you are not sure that a particular agency can help you, call and explain what information or help you are trying to locate. Staff persons will usually know where to direct you if they cannot help you.

A growing network of treatment centers and recovery groups has resources available for families. You can contact counseling offices, treatment centers, or universities and usually get leads about people, groups, and organizations that assist families in specific ways.

You can call the offices of radio talk shows. Radio talk programs have to keep an extensive listing of guests who address various topics. They will probably have a list of referrals to groups and organizations as well.

The best resources are human resources. Within your community, there are educational seminars, men's groups, recovery groups, parenting groups, church groups, school-related groups, and so on. To tap into these meetings, you can contact your local Chamber of Commerce.

The real key to finding information and resources is to persevere. Once you know what you want to accomplish, what tasks you need to complete to reach your goals, what information or help you lack, it's just a matter of dogged pursuit until you get what you need.

PERSONAL EVALUATION

- When have you reached out to find further knowledge or help in a specific aspect of fathering?
- How do you feel about consulting with others regarding fathering issues?

ACTION

Review the goals you've written in your notebook. To achieve those goals, you will need knowledge, practical help, and support. Identify every area where you need input from others. Add a section to your notebook titled "Help." Transfer the goals you have already chosen, and follow each with a list of what you will need help to know, understand, do, and continue doing. List the people, groups, and organizations whose cooperation you will seek.

After you have completed the list, flip back through the pages of this book, and list other areas of interest where you will need help to continue growing as a father and as a person.

Make a list of possible consultants: books, experts, other fathers, your children's mother, friends, clergy, and so on. Decide the first three things you will do to get the help and knowledge you need to reach the objectives for this journey. Do one of them today.

REFLECTION

What help did you find by calling on others more knowledgeable than yourself? How did you feel about doing this? What might be influencing your feelings about consulting others with regard to fathering issues?

ENCOURAGEMENT

Admitting your need for knowledge and assistance gives you greater power to provide for the needs of your family.

FOOD FOR THOUGHT

Training a baby by the book is a good idea, only you need a different book for each baby.

—Dan Bennett

Planning for Growth and Development

Your children will grow up. As they do, you must continue to adapt your fathering to meet their needs at each stage of development. A world-class father plans ahead to accommodate the changing needs of his children. When your child is born, he or she is completely dependent upon the loving care of others for survival. Each child has a unique personality, but all children share a need for discipline, socialization, and guidance. It is in your home, under your protection, that your children will learn how to live. Planning ahead for each stage of development will make you more effective in your fathering.

Childhood can be considered in terms of infancy (birth to age two), preschool (ages two to five), middle childhood (ages six to twelve), and adolescence (thirteen to eighteen). At each stage of childhood, and also during young adulthood, children need different things from their parents. In the years prior to adolescence, your children need limits, guidance, discipline, affection, and close attention. During these early years, they need you to tell them exactly what to do, how to do it, what to think, what to wear, and when to go bed; in short, they need you to define the boundary lines of their lives and fill in all the colors.

As they reach various stages (particularly around age two and entering adolescence), they will strongly test the boundaries you have established to see how well they will be enforced and what life would be like without them. This testing is part of the process that will allow them to establish and uphold their own boundaries as adults.

You would be wise to become familiar with the basic developmental tasks for each stage of growth. Once you understand the tasks being accomplished during particular phases, you will be in a better position to guide your children successfully through each stage.

Consider this example from Dr. James Dobson's book *Dr. Dobson Answers Your Questions*. The question is, "Are the 'terrible twos' really so terrible?" Part of the answer follows,

> If there is one word that characterizes the period between fifteen and twenty-four months of age, it is no! No, he doesn't want to eat his cereal. No, he doesn't want to play with his dump truck. No, he doesn't want to take his bath. And you can be sure, no, he doesn't want to go to bed anytime at all.

You may find yourself at a disadvantage if you don't have this understanding about what to expect when your children enter this stage of development. You may be overly critical of your parenting ability or of the children. During the early years, they need guidance and firm controls. During adolescence, your children will be developing their own values and defining their individual identities. As they wrestle with this task, they need you to be there more as a sounding board to test their theories about life. During adolescence, they need you to release control by degrees while being available for support as they try their wings.

If you neglect providing firm discipline and abundant guidance during the early years or try to completely control them during adolescence, you will be out of sync with the stage of development they are experiencing. And you will be at odds with the children in unnecessary ways. Understanding what to expect of each stage of development, which developmental tasks each child is working through, and what you can do to parent your children during each stage will give you a greater sense of confidence.

PERSONAL EVALUATION

- What do you know about the typical patterns for each stage of child development?
- Have you ever experienced frustration with some aspect of your children's behavior that was alleviated by learning something about the particular stage of development they were going through at the time?
- Do you see how understanding something about human development could give you an advantage in fathering?

ACTION

Draw a time line starting with the current year. Place marks at five-year intervals for the next twenty years. In a column at the left margin of the paper, write the names of your children. Under the mark for the current year and across from the child's name, place the age of that child. Project each child's age for the years marked. For example:

Child's Name	1992	1997	2002	2007	2012
Casey	7	12	17	22	27
Taylor	2	7	12	17	22
Haley	1	6	11	16	21

Taking into consideration the developmental stages of each of your children, plan the following for each year on your time line:

- What developmental stages do you need to understand and prepare for before your children reach each of the designated years?
- What financial plans do you need to make to be able to provide for the emerging needs of children this age?
- What changes would you like to work toward in terms of your career position and work schedule to accommodate the needs of your children at these ages?
- What other elements of life do you want to plan or anticipate to meet the changing needs of your family?

This week visit your local bookstore or library, get at least one book related to the developmental stages of your children, and begin reading it.

REFLECTION

Do you feel that you were prepared for the present stages of development of your children? How does it feel to look ahead and anticipate your children's growth? As they grow, can you see yourself growing and maturing to parent them well?

ENCOURAGEMENT

In his book *The Tunnel of Love*, Peter De Vries points out, "Who of us is mature enough for offspring before the offspring themselves arrive? The value of marriage is not that adults produce children but that children produce adults." It is part of God's plan to use growing children to encourage maturity in the life of the parent. By planning ahead for your children's development, you are contributing to your personal growth as well as theirs.

FOOD FOR THOUGHT

There are only two lasting bequests we can hope to give our children. One of these is roots; the other, wings.

—Hodding Carter

Investing in the Lives of Your Children

Every man must choose how he will invest himself in this life. Your choices about how to invest your time, energies, finances, and your own soul set the parameters of your life and where your contributions will cause growth. Given the fact that you operate with a limited supply of time, energy, and money, these choices are often difficult. There is only so much of you to go around, and you may feel that there's not enough to satisfy all the demands placed on you. However, wise investments hold out the promise of abundant rewards.

A Hebrew proverb says, "Great is work which lends dignity to a man." One of man's greatest sources of dignity is found in productive and rewarding work. The motivation for devoting yourself to your work is not only to succeed financially but also to succeed in your own eyes as a man. Productive work allows you to provide for the needs of your family. It's understandable that work requires a substantial personal investment. However, your children need much more than your paycheck; they need you to invest directly in their lives as well.

There is no greater work than investing in the lives of your children. If you are investing so much of yourself at the workplace that there's not much left to invest at home, you will experience some very real losses in the future when you see your investments come to fruition. Your children are growing. Their lives are available for your investment every day. Each day, each choice you make about where to place the use of your time, attention, affection, energy, emotional involvement, and finances determines where your life will have a positive impact and where your rewards will be in the future.

The goal is to find a balance in diversifying your investments at work and at home. In this way you win all the way around. You may need to redistribute your life somewhat, perhaps even taking some short-term losses in your career. However, you and your children will reap benefits of your involvement in their lives, which will continue to pay off for generations.

Before you can determine if you need to redistribute your personal investments, you must first have an accurate assessment of where you are currently giving of yourself. Evaluate where you are investing yourself in the following categories: time, energy, emotional involvement, and finances.

Time

In our fast-paced society, time is a valuable commodity. Children may not understand all the demands on your time or your reasons for deciding how to use your time. They do understand that you spend your time on those things important to you. The time you spend with your children is every bit as valuable to them as it is to you; to them, it reflects their value in your life.

Energy

We all have peak energy times when we are at our best, times when we are moderately tired, and times when we are exhausted. Note how much time you have with your children and the quality of that time based on your energy level.

Emotional Involvement

Emotional contact would involve sharing emotion-packed moments with your children: giving warm hugs, comforting them when they are sad or hurt, listening or assisting as they work out angry feelings, affirming them when they are insecure or critical of themselves, laughing together, sharing excitement, and so on.

Finances

The way you choose to use and invest the finances at your disposal influences how you are able to invest in your children's lives directly.

PERSONAL EVALUATION

Time

- How much time do you think you spend involved with your children daily and weekly? (Do not include times when you are in the same room but emotionally unavailable.)

Energy

- When do you tend to have your peak energy times?
- When you do have time to spend with your children, how often are you at your peak energy level while with them?
- How often are you exhausted while spending time with your children? (Do not count being exhausted *after* spending time with them.)
- Apart from work, what other activities and relationships draw on your supply of energy?

Emotional Involvement

- How often do you connect emotionally with your children in an affirming way?
- Is your emotional involvement with their lives a one-way operation, sending them emotional communication (anger, approval, acceptance, sadness, pride, disappointment, and so on) without allowing them to communicate a range of emotions back to you?
- Would your children feel close enough with you to talk about something that was upsetting them emotionally?

Finances

- Do you rely on buying things for your children to compensate for what you may not invest personally in their lives?
- Do you manage your finances in such a way that your children's well-being is a priority?

ACTION

Perhaps you have never given much thought to these investments. It's easy to assume that since you are living with others, you are going to automatically invest in their lives. Today's action step will help clarify your estimations of where your investments are really going. Create the following form to be included in your notebook. Across the top write these headings with columns beneath them:

Date	Time	Energy Level	Energy Spent	Hugs	Emotional Connections	Money

- In the "Date" column, write down the dates for the remaining fourteen days of your journey. Take a few moments at the end of each day to review your real investment in your children's lives in these various categories.
- In the "Time" column, note how much time you spent interacting or involved directly with your children.
- In the "Energy Level" column, note whether your energy level was peak, moderate, or exhausted during the time with them.
- In the "Energy Spent" column, note any activity you did for your children's well-being that required energy (apart from work) and the amount of time spent. (For example, you would note taking your daily journey as energy spent for your children's well-being, although it wasn't spent with them.)

- In the "Hugs" column, note the number of times you hugged your children or otherwise gave them physical affection.
- In the "Emotional Connections" column, note how many times you were able to connect with your children during emotion-packed moments.
- In the "Money" column, note how much money you invested directly into their lives.

REFLECTION

Are you looking forward to keeping track of these investments over the next two weeks, or are you feeling resistant? Are you feeling defensive? If you are, what might you be trying to defend against?

ENCOURAGEMENT

It is not easy to maintain balance in choosing how to invest your life. Your willingness to look at your life honestly from this perspective gives you a greater opportunity to invest wisely and reap the rewards of investing in your family.

FOOD FOR THOUGHT

Great things cannot be bought for small sums.

The Costs, Rewards, and Risks of Investing

When considering any investment, you must answer a few basic questions before making a wise decision. You need to know the costs, the potential rewards, and the risks involved. If you are convinced the potential rewards warrant taking the risks involved, you are left to consider whether you can afford what it costs. If an investment looks particularly attractive but you couldn't afford the cost, you might be inclined to find ways to get the necessary resources. You might draw from other assets or redistribute your holdings to take advantage of an important opportunity that would otherwise be missed.

This process is basically the same when considering what to invest in the lives of your children. The opportunity to invest won't remain open indefinitely. If you choose not to invest in your children, a day will come when they will look elsewhere for those who will meet their heartfelt needs. At that point the window of opportunity may close.

Rewards are easier to weigh if you can add them up in a column, project the returns over the course of years, and come up with some figure that would quantify what you are hoping to gain. It doesn't work that way in human relationships. Some rewards may be relational, such as enjoying the love and trust of your children as they grow up. Some rewards may be ethereal, such as having the confidence that your children will spend eternity in heaven. Some rewards may be tangible, such as seeing your children achieve their goals in the profession of their choice or seeing them become financially independent.

There is no guarantee that being more involved in your children's lives will spare them difficulties, but you will have a much greater opportunity to help them avoid pitfalls than the father who has invested his life elsewhere.

The risks include the possibility that you could invest fully of yourself in their lives and find even your best efforts are lacking or rejected. What if you offer them the best that is in you, and that ends up being something they despise? If you remember the youth rebellion of the 1960s, you may have wondered what it would be like to be on the receiving end of that type of rebellion against parents.

Another risk is that you may lose out on some professional advantages given to those who belong heart, soul, mind, and body to their companies. Competition is fierce in the workplace. If you decide to invest more of yourself in your family, you shouldn't expect the ones who are losing a portion of your attention to applaud your decision. The number one *New York Times* best-seller *A Passion for Excellence,* by Tom Peters and Nancy Austin, points out this fact. The authors say,

> We are frequently asked if it is possible to "have it all"—a full and satisfying personal life and a full and

satisfying, hard-working, professional one. Our answer is: No. The price of excellence is time, energy, attention, and focus, at the very same time that energy, attention, and focus could have gone toward enjoying your daughter's soccer game. Excellence is a high cost item. As David Ogilvy observed in *Confessions of an Advertising Man:* "If you prefer to spend all your spare time growing roses or playing with your children, I like you better, but do not complain that you are not being promoted fast enough."

The costs of investing in your children's lives may be measured in experiencing daily distractions, having patience tested to the limit, looking at yourself honestly, being willing to deal with personal problems, and making a host of other good choices for the sake of your family. Doing what is best for your family may not be the most comfortable choice for you at the moment. The costs are measured in the kind of love that bears all things, believes the best of your children, and endures the slings and arrows known by anyone who dares to love with all his heart.

If you are like many other men, the time, energy, attention, and focus called for will probably not come from a surplus account. Most men are already taxed to the limit. You will need to carefully weigh your priorities and see how you can adjust your life at this time to invest what you would like in your children's lives. If your circumstances are such that you can't invest directly in their lives to the degree that you would like, you can determine what factors are within your control to change in the long run and come up with a plan to move in that direction.

PERSONAL EVALUATION

- What are all the rewards you can think of (immediate and long-term) that could result from greater direct investment in your children's lives?
- What are the risks you take by investing in your children's lives?
- What are the risks you take by *not* investing in your children's lives?
- What would be the immediate and long-term costs to change your life-style to enable you to invest more fully in your children's lives?

ACTION

In your notebook make a list for each: the costs, rewards, and risks of investing. Weigh your options and decide if you will redistribute your resources to be able to invest more directly in your children's lives. If you decide to redistribute your resources, describe precisely what changes you will make immediately and eventually.

REFLECTION

Do you wish you could invest more but find the costs prohibitive at this time? What would it take to make you able to afford to invest more fully in your children's lives? Do you appreciate the value of what you have already invested in their lives?

ENCOURAGEMENT

You are investing yourself in the lives of your children, or you would not have spent the time, energy, and attention required to come this far in your journey. You can only do the best you can do. Once you have given these issues careful consideration and made the greatest level of investment you can for now, acknowledge that as progress in the right direction. In time you can work toward increasing your level of investment.

FOOD FOR THOUGHT

Becoming a father is easy enough.
But being one can be rough.
    —William Busch
        quoted from *Father: The Figure and the Force*

Preparing for Life's Emergencies

Children living in southern California are taught that an earthquake of substantial magnitude could occur suddenly at any time. Schools throughout the state practice emergency preparedness, since all children in the danger zone are at risk. By practicing what to do in case of emergency, they significantly increase their chances of remaining safe. I witnessed an earthquake drill at my daughter's elementary school. The forethought and leadership displayed by the principal and staff provide an example of the leadership you can take to protect your children from life's emergencies.

When the alarm sounded, the children took cover and counted aloud together to one hundred. At the all-clear signal they formed two lines, walking away from buildings and electrical wiring, to the playground where the principal was accounting for every class. The children in each class knew where they belonged because plans had been made and clearly communicated to them in advance.

The children quieted themselves so they could hear Mr. Pierce, the principal. He commended them for following the rules and responding as they had been taught. All eyes were focused on him as he spoke. "It is very important that you practice as though this were a real emergency," he said, "because your lives may depend on how well prepared you are." The children took the drill seriously because they understood the concern for their safety, even if they didn't fully understand the danger.

In case of a real emergency, the principal and staff are well prepared. They have a stockpile of food, water, and emergency supplies and a plan for the immediate crisis and long-term care of the children. The attention devoted to emergency preparedness gives the children a sense of security in a world where danger is a reality.

Although the fact is uncomfortable to consider, children today are growing up in a world that can be a dangerous place. You exercise your love and leadership by practicing emergency preparedness with them. The children who perform earthquake drills don't worry constantly about earthquakes; they know that someone who cares for them has planned to ensure their safety. By acknowledging and preparing for the dangers your children face, you can give them a greater sense of security.

PERSONAL EVALUATION

- Have you given much thought to the dangers and risks your children face?
- What have you taught your children to do to protect themselves from potential dangers?
- Have you educated yourself on how to prepare your children to avoid risk and deal with dangers that may face them as they grow up?

ACTION

Provide your children with knowledge of the risks, a plan to handle the danger (what they are to do, where they are to turn for help, and so on), and a commitment to be there to get them through any crisis. The following dangers represent real risks for your children. You may think of others that pertain to your particular situation. Write these headings at the top of a page in your notebook:

Danger	Knowledge	Preparation	Plan	Promise	Age

In the "Danger" column, list drug abuse, alcohol abuse, AIDS, negative peer pressure, sexually transmitted disease, child abuse, molestation, problems adjusting to puberty, poisons, and any others you choose. Place a check in the appropriate column if you *know* about this topic and how to protect your children, you have *prepared* them by explaining the danger and how to avoid it, you have given them *planned* instructions of what to do if this occurs, and you have given them your *promise* that in case of emergency they can come to you for help and protection. In the "Age" column, note the *age* you think it appropriate to begin preparing them for this danger.

REFLECTION

Which dangers do you feel uncomfortable considering? How do you plan to overcome your discomfort to be able to preserve your children's safety? Are there any dangers you wish your parents had prepared you for in advance?

ENCOURAGEMENT

You can't make the world completely safe, but you can take steps that will go a long way toward protecting your children. You also demonstrate your love by letting them know you are there for them, even during the times when life is frightening.

FOOD FOR THOUGHT

Give me a newborn child, and in ten years I can have him so scared he'll never dare lift his voice above a whisper, or so brave that he'll fear nothing.
—Dr. George A. Dorsey

Rescheduling Your Life

It has been said that time is money. In our society, time is certainly one of our most valuable commodities. Americans will pay significant sums for anything that will save them time. This emphasis on the value of time doesn't escape the notice of your children. When you choose to reschedule your life to reflect your desire to be a world-class father, your children will realize their true value to you in a way that goes beyond mere words or things that you can buy them.

You have already established your responsibilities, priorities, and objectives with regard to fathering. Reconsidering your fathering role means rethinking the distribution of time under your control. Since you probably don't have much spare time, you'll need to eliminate some activities that are unnecessary or less important than your newly focused priorities. You'll need to make room in your calendar to accommodate any new commitments.

PERSONAL EVALUATION

- Does your current schedule reflect the time you want to spend being more directly involved in your children's lives?
- Are there some commitments you have taken on

yourself outside your fathering role that could be delegated to others?
- Are you willing to make scheduling changes to enhance your involvement in your children's lives?

ACTION

Chronicle the hours in your days for the next ten days. Your goal is to mold your schedule to fit the shape of your true values.

Step One

Sketch a diagram that depicts twenty-four hours for each day in the coming ten days (if you already keep a calendar, refer to the plans you have recorded for the next two weeks).

Step Two

Fill in the hours that you regularly spend sleeping, eating, grooming, and taking care of other physical necessities.

Step Three

Fill in the hours that are already committed to on-going activities that you are not in a position to change, such as school, work, church, and so on.

Step Four

Fill in all of the appointments you have planned for the next ten days, such as going to the dentist or attending meetings, sporting events, social events, and so on.

Anything left open on your calendar should represent areas of opportunity: opportunities to fulfill your responsibilities, to take care of yourself, and to move in the direction of achieving your goals for your family.

Step Five

Make a list of the things that you now need to do and/or want to do in the coming ten days. Be sure to consider having regular family meeting times and one-on-one time with each child, taking one of your children along with you for some activities, reading, and so on.

Step Six

Read over the list, and rank each item with a $V =$ very important to me, $M =$ moderately important to me, or $O =$ optional (not really important to me). Reconsider what is truly important in light of your current focus on being a world-class father.

Step Seven

Turn your short-term goals into commitments by taking them from the list of random items on your floating "to do" list and scheduling them into your daily calendar as appointments. If they do not fit into appointed times, commit them to a specific day, such as Thursday afternoon or evening.

This commitment should be realistic, or you will

become discouraged. A small improvement that is within reach is better than an idealistic calendar that will prove overwhelming. If your schedule is too tight, you can adjust the application of your goals into somewhat shorter time segments, spread out over a longer course of time.

REFLECTION

Are you excited about whatever changes you are able to make in the right direction, or are you feeling somewhat guilty that you can't do more to be directly involved with your children?

ENCOURAGEMENT

Remember, changing your schedule is a major undertaking. Your commitment to positive changes and follow-through will make a difference as they are repeated over the course of days, months, and years.

FOOD FOR THOUGHT

One way to curb delinquency is to take parents off the streets at night.

—Morrie Gallint

Enjoying Your Children

Enjoying your children is one of the prime benefits of fatherhood. However, it is not something that comes naturally to all fathers, especially those who raise children in a time-conscious culture such as ours. Taking time to enjoy your children may be something you have to cultivate. You may have to overcome some of your preconceived notions about what a father is supposed to do so that you will be free to simply enjoy your children.

The Walt Disney classic *Mary Poppins* has long been a favorite with children. You may be surprised to find out that the story is about the transformation of a father (one who prides himself on being world-class), who discovers how to enjoy his children. Mr. Banks is consumed with his career. He rules over his home, provides well, and seeks to make sure his two children are raised properly.

At the beginning of the story Mr. Banks is perturbed when the children keep getting lost while flying their kites. It would never cross his mind to fly kites with them. He seems unable to appreciate their playfulness or the comedy of their childish mischief. He completely misses their invitations for him to play with them. Through the help of Mary Poppins, Mr. Banks finally recognizes what he has been missing and summons the courage to simply enjoy his kids. The film ends with father and children running off together to fly kites. The faces of father and children are filled with the joy and excitement that were out of reach for Mr. Banks at the beginning of the story.

In his book *Childhood*, Bill Cosby writes, "It is popular today to say that we have to find the child within us. For me, this would be a short search." Bill Cosby is a man who obviously enjoys life, perhaps because he never lost sight of the enjoyment and richness children can bring to life.

You, too, can find a wealth of joy in living if you will allow yourself the privilege of fully enjoying your children. You don't need Mary Poppins to miraculously cause you to reexamine your priorities. You can do that for yourself. Your reward will be the freedom to play, to rediscover childlike excitement, to explore life from a brighter perspective.

There are a host of ways to enjoy your children. You can enjoy watching them. Watch them as they play. Take a walk with them, and allow them to be your guides. It may seem to take forever as they explore every leaf and bug along the way. Notice how they are not driven by time constraints the way adults are. Try watching them as they watch a movie. Focus your attention on their facial expressions as they register a wide range of emotions. Watch them grow wide-eyed, smile, and laugh. Watch them as they sleep. When you take the time to watch your children, you will find a great source of joy for your soul.

You can also enjoy playing with them. Read them

stories. Let them read you stories. Lie on the floor and let them crawl on you. Wrestle; play tag; give horseback rides. Play word games and board games with them. Join in their games. Teach them some of the games you enjoyed as a child. Take off your wristwatch and go fly kites with them. Build something, cook something, explore a secret hiding place, swing on the playground swing set, slide down a slide, throw a ball, or ride a bike.

PERSONAL EVALUATION

- In the last month what have you done that allowed you to enjoy watching your children?
- What have you done in the last month that allowed you to enjoy playing with your children? How much time did you spend having fun with your children this week?
- What games did you enjoy as a child that you can pass on to your children?

ACTION

Spend some time today watching your children at play.

Schedule a block of time to play with your children this week.

Get down on the floor at their level and physically play with your children for at least half an hour.

Optional: Rent the video of *Mary Poppins*, and watch it with your children. Then go fly a kite with them.

REFLECTION

Having children gives you wonderful opportunities to enjoy the simple pleasures of life if you will allow yourself. How often do you allow yourself the pleasure of enjoying your children? How did it feel when you did allow yourself to have fun with them? What keeps you from doing so more often?

ENCOURAGEMENT

You deserve some fun in life! The time you spend playing with your children is not wasted. It means more to them than you will probably ever realize.

FOOD FOR THOUGHT

Happy is he that is happy in his children.
—Anonymous

To show a child what has once delighted you, to find the child's delight added to your own, so that there is now a double delight seen in the glow of trust and affection, this is happiness.
—J. B. Priestly
Delight

The Man Behind the Title

To be a world-class father, you need to experience the balanced life of a whole person, not just focus on the part of your life related to your children. Your children see you not only as a father but as a role model for what it means to be a good man. It has been said that what you are speaks louder than what you say. Part of your journey involves considering how you are doing as a man, beyond your role as father.

Every man is a triune being—body, mind, and spirit. To preserve your health, you need to care for yourself in each of these ways. Make sure that your basic health needs are being met so that you will be able to continue to care for your children. Physically, you need to get a healthy balanced diet, plenty of exercise, and enough rest to replenish your strength. Mentally, you need to continue to learn new things. You need to clean out any mental trash and negative attitudes that draw you downward to a lower level of being. Spiritually, you need to be at peace with yourself and God. You need to find the inner satisfaction that dispels the hunger that can lead you into trouble.

Your love for your children can be a powerful force, motivating you to seek wholeness and health for their sake. It's amazing how differently you may see yourself when you consider how your children would see you if they knew you as you are in the secret depths of your heart. Dwight L. Moody said, "Character is what you are in the dark."

An amazing thing happens when you live with your children. They see you at your best and at your worst. Your children may be part of God's plan to get you to consider the transformation that could make you at peace with yourself, even in the dark.

PERSONAL EVALUATION

- How do you take care of yourself in the following ways: physically, spiritually, and intellectually?
- Do you feel at peace with yourself and God?
- Do you feel satisfied with your life and relationships?
- Do you feel comfortable enough with your "private self" that you are not afraid to allow your children to be close to you?
- How have becoming a father and loving your children caused you to want to become a man of excellent character?

ACTION

Across the top of one page in your notebook, write "Body," "Mind," and "Spirit." In the column under each one, note how well you feel you are doing in taking care of that aspect of your being: poor, fair, good, or excellent. Also in each column, list what you do to nurture yourself in each area.

On another sheet in your notebook, write "Public

Self" and "Private Self." In each column, write a description of the man others know you to be publicly and the man you know yourself to be privately. At the bottom of this sheet, list anything you are hiding in your private world that you would like to be free of.

Think of one thing you could do for each area of your life to make you a healthier, more balanced person. Schedule them into your calendar for the coming week.

If something in your private life or your spiritual life needs care, consider talking with someone you respect as having a healthy spiritual life or a counselor who could help you sort out the issues and move toward greater health.

REFLECTION

Are you comfortable with the man you are today? How can your love for your children have a positive influence on you as a whole person?

ENCOURAGEMENT

Thoughtful consideration of your life can open the door to transformation, deep satisfaction, and wholeness.

FOOD FOR THOUGHT

The virtue of parents is a great dowry.
—Latin Proverb

Learning from Your Father

A Gypsy proverb declares, "You have to dig deep to bury your daddy." This saying captures the truth that fathers have a profound impact on their children. Whether your father was a tower of virtue, whose image inspires you to greatness, or a man whose life was replete with flaws, you can learn from his life if you are willing to dig deep into your own soul.

Developing an attitude that can find good in your father's life and learn from it is a choice you make. It doesn't hinge on how well your father performed his role or how good your relationship was or is with him. You need only a positive attitude that allows you to find whatever good there is, acknowledge what wasn't good, and deal with both in a positive way. You can choose to acknowledge what your father did right as well as learn from where he failed to live up to your expectations. You can exercise gratitude for the love you find, even if it wasn't always communicated perfectly.

Your father may have fulfilled his responsibilities well, developed a loving, supportive relationship with you, and raised you so that you were prepared to face life confidently on your own when the time came. If that is the case, you can probably see the positive effects your father's life has had on you. If your father failed in these respects, you may wonder what it means about you, that your own father treated you in such a way. In reality, any failing of your father says more about him than it does about you. However, the perceptions we adopt as children often form the basis for an erroneous self-image as adults.

A human being may fail in countless ways. When that human being is your father, and the failing concerns meeting your needs, you tend to feel the pain of that failure to the core of your being. Perhaps your father didn't give you the care and attention you needed, hurt you, rejected you, or constantly criticized you. Perhaps he died when you were young or wasn't there for you for some other reason. Maybe he was consumed by some form of addiction or compulsion that made him emotionally unavailable. Whatever the particular circumstances in your life, disappointment in relationship with your father can cultivate deep pain and self-doubt. You can confront and resolve these disappointments and the resulting resentments in a healthy way.

PERSONAL EVALUATION

- Have you been able to take responsibility for your own life, regardless of how well or poorly your father took care of you?
- Are you caught in a power struggle, still fighting some battle with your father? What do you think the roots and issues of that battle might be? What can you learn from the struggle?
- What assumptions have you made about your-

97

self, based on the ways your father treated you as a child? Considering these assumptions from an adult perspective, do you question the validity of some of them?

ACTION

List everything good you see in your father's life that you would like to emulate.

List the downfalls you see in your father's life along with the positive lessons you can draw from his shortcomings.

List everything you can think of that you are grateful for in your father's life and his relationship with you over the years.

List times when you feel he tried his best to take care of your needs, even if his attempts weren't fully successful.

If there is current pain in your life because of your relationship with your father, go through the following process:

- List the offenses you hold against your father.
- Acknowledge the validity of the pain they caused in your life.
- Admit any feelings that those offenses should be paid for in some way.
- Make a conscious choice to clear the debt you are holding against him. (This step is for your sake. Unresolved bitterness eats away at you.) Consider the times you have been in need of for-

giveness; try to extend to him the same grace you would hope for yourself.
- Clarify those things you either appreciate most or most wish for in your relationship with your father. Turn those around into commitments of what you will be sure to include in relationship with your children.

If your relationship with your father represents an ongoing struggle that interferes with your ability to function as the father you want to be, consider discussing the issue with a professional family therapist.

REFLECTION

Given your relationship with your father and the history of your relationship, do you think there is anything within your power that can be done to develop the kind of relationship you desire?

ENCOURAGEMENT

By processing your feelings toward your father, you are able to improve your relationship with your children.

FOOD FOR THOUGHT

Only the brave know how to forgive.
                              —Ancient Proverb

Maximizing Your Assets

Whoever you are, you have assets to work with. You have strengths of character, spiritual resources, talents, understanding, experience, physical and mental abilities. All of them are available for you to draw upon in being a world-class father. To make the most of your assets, you must take an inventory of your assets, and consider how you can best use them to accomplish what you want within your family relationships. If you focus on what you lack rather than what you have, you will be severely limited from achieving your best.

I recently heard a story of a surgeon who had done a tour of duty in Vietnam. The other surgeons who had been in the medical emergency unit for a length of time before he arrived had adopted the practice of working first to save those who could be saved quickly, since they were overrun with severely injured soldiers. They did not devote several hours of precious time to save the life of someone who was severely mutilated because it could mean the loss of many other lives in the meantime. When the new recruit arrived for his first shift, he was horrified at the task before him. He began work on a nineteen-year-old who had lost both legs and both eyes. He refused to let that young man die, despite the advice of the other medics. For seven grueling hours he patched the young man back together and saved his life.

In the months and years that followed, the surgeon grew to understand the reasons behind the advice given by his battle-hardened comrades, who tried to divert him from his heroic efforts. They saw the young man as only half a man, whose life wasn't worth saving under the circumstances. After the war, the surgeon was tormented with guilt over what might have become of the man whose life he saved. Was he wasting away in some veterans' hospital, suffering with bed sores, filled with loneliness? Did he now pray to God that he had not been saved? Did he curse the surgeon who had consigned him to life without sight or legs? The surgeon dared not know the answers.

After twenty-five years, the surgeon was put in contact with the man he had saved that first day in the jungles of Vietnam. The man had triumphed in life. He had always believed that whoever had worked so hard to save his life must have seen something worth saving. The young man adopted an attitude that focused on what he had to work with, not what was missing. He was happily married and the proud father of three well-adjusted children. He had devoted himself to teaching those with handicaps how to face life by maximizing their assets rather than bemoaning their limitations.

This man's story shows that regardless of what may be missing from your life, you have a great deal to work with. Life itself gives hope. Each new day brings the potential of bringing out the best in yourself and others. If you are willing to focus on your assets and use them to the best of your ability, you can be a world-class father.

PERSONAL EVALUATION

- Do you tend to focus on your assets or your limitations when considering your life?
- Are you willing to consider your assets, even if that is not the way you usually look at yourself?

ACTION

Make a list of all your assets. Include your strengths of character, such as honesty, diligence, perseverance, kindness, loyalty, patience, self-control, being hardworking, and the like. Even if you perceive these strengths to a small degree, the fact that they are there at all gives you something to work with. If nurtured, these qualities can grow.

List your talents and abilities: physical, mental, artistic, personal, professional, athletic, and so on.

List areas where you have understanding and experience.

List your spiritual, material, and financial assets.

Consider how all of these assets could be brought into play to make you a world-class father. Summarize your thoughts; name three ways you could use your assets to positively affect your fathering role and relationships. List these three action steps in your notebook. Do one of these things today that maximizes the use of your assets in being a world-class father.

REFLECTION

Are you surprised to see how much you have to work with to enhance your own life and relationships with your children?

How does it feel to think of yourself in such positive terms? Do you need to focus more consistently on making the most of what you have rather than dwelling on what you lack?

ENCOURAGEMENT

Most people take for granted the assets they have at their disposal. By making yourself aware of your assets, you are in a much better position to make the most of them.

FOOD FOR THOUGHT

The first step to raising positive kids is to become a positive parent.
—Zig Ziglar
Raising Positive Kids in a Negative World

Dealing with Drawbacks

Job applicants are often asked in an interview, "Tell me about your greatest weakness." An understanding in business settings is that you can learn about people by seeing how they deal with their drawbacks. Do they recognize that they have weaknesses? Are they evasive? Are they able to honestly cope with personal limitations from a positive perspective? In the interview setting the weaknesses and how the person is able to integrate the weaknesses into the overall fabric of life are considered.

Every human being has both strengths and weaknesses, assets and liabilities, advantages and drawbacks. How you deal with your drawbacks will have an impact on being a world-class father. Let's define a *drawback* as anything in your life that interferes with your ability to be the kind of father you aspire to be or to live life to the fullest. It could be something outside yourself, such as a job that demands frequent absences from your family. It could be a personal problem, such as a violent temper or an addiction. It could be a medical problem that would limit your ability to play with your children. How are you to deal with these drawbacks that represent real interference with being a father?

The first key is to face the drawback honestly. It does no good for anyone to pretend that there is not a problem when there is one. Denial can be a defense mechanism. It may help you keep your distance from the pain of having to face your drawbacks and the problems they cause. Denial does nothing to have a genuine, positive effect on your life. You need to honestly see what the problems are, what impact they are having on your family, what you can possibly do to deal with the problems, and how you can get the help you need.

The second key is to practice the truth captured in the Serenity Prayer. This prayer has been adopted by various twelve-step groups. It says "God, grant me the serenity to accept the things I cannot change, the courage to change the things I can, and the wisdom to know the difference. Amen."

For each drawback you recognize in your life, determine if it is something you can change. If it is, summon the courage to do whatever you can to make those changes. If it is something beyond your control, accept the reality of your life and make the most of it.

Drawbacks in life are best dealt with in daily doses. Learn to take life one day at a time, especially when you are dealing with the areas of life that you consider to be weaknesses. You can't go back and change yesterday. You don't know what tomorrow will bring. The best you can do is to live the present moment to the best of your ability.

PERSONAL EVALUATION

- If you were being interviewed about being a father and were asked, "Tell me about your greatest weakness," how would you reply?

- Do you feel uncomfortable acknowledging draw-backs that limit your fathering? If you do, why do you think that is?

ACTION

In your notebook, list three things that are draw-backs to being a world-class father, and take each through the following process.

1. Define the drawback.

2. Answer these questions: To what degree do you stay in denial regarding this issue? How do you pre-tend that it isn't really as much of a problem as it is? How do you react when other family members mention this problem?

3. Describe how this drawback affects each member of your family. You may need to ask them how they are affected, since they may not show you the full impact it has had on them.

4. List the options to deal with this drawback. After each option, note if you are willing to pursue it or not, and include your reasons for your decision.

5. If it is something you can change, state how you will need to exercise courage to make the necessary changes.

6. If it is something you cannot change, list ways you could possibly compensate for what is lacking.

7. Define what you can do today to deal with this drawback. Do it today.

8. Determine to live with this drawback one day at a time.

If you feel able, discuss the three drawbacks you

choose with your wife or children (if they are of an appropriate age) and what you are considering to deal with these drawbacks.

REFLECTION

Did thinking through this process give you a handle on dealing with your drawbacks?

How did it feel to consider sharing or to actually share this difficult process with those you love?

Do you have hope that you can integrate dealing with your weaknesses into the fabric of your life and still be a world-class father?

ENCOURAGEMENT

You are not alone. Everyone has weaknesses and drawbacks. In our culture men are raised to hide their weaknesses rather than deal with them openly. By demonstrating the courage and honesty to face whatever drawbacks you see in your life, you will open avenues of help that will allow you to be a world-class father and to enjoy life in the process.

FOOD FOR THOUGHT

The wound that bleeds inwardly is the most dangerous.

—Anonymous

Keeping Communication Lines Open

Good communication makes for good relationships. If communication breaks down, soon the relationships dissolve as well. Consider the biblical account of the building of the Tower of Babel. The whole earth had one language and one speech, the writer of Genesis tells us. And the people said, "Come, let us build ourselves a city, and a tower whose top is in the heavens; let us make a name for ourselves, lest we be scattered abroad over the face of the whole earth" (Gen. 11:4). Apparently, God didn't think they had such a good idea, but He did realize the power of clear communication in conjunction with a well-defined goal:

> And the LORD said, "Indeed the people are one and they all have one language, and this is what they begin to do; now nothing that they propose to do will be withheld from them. Come, let Us go down and there confuse their language, that they may not understand one another's speech." So the LORD scattered them abroad from there over the face of all the earth, and they ceased building the city (Gen. 11:6–8).

When the people had one purpose and one language being clearly communicated and clearly understood by all, nothing could stop them from achieving their purpose. When confusion arose in their language and they didn't understand one another's speech, they scattered. They ceased building because there was no point in trying to work together if they couldn't understand one another. Instead they turned to those who could understand them.

These truths apply directly to your family. If you and your children lose the ability to speak the same language, your children will scatter and turn to those who seem to understand them. The good plans you have for building up their lives cannot proceed without good communication.

Good communication involves sending messages (verbal and nonverbal), listening, and giving and receiving feedback. To be a world-class father, you need to practice good communication in all these areas.

Sending Messages

Make clear statements so that a child can understand precisely what you mean. The younger the child, the more precise the parent has to be in communication. In addressing a young child, you do better to say, "Pick up your toys and put them in the toy box," than to say, "Go clean your room." A precise message also leaves less room for misunderstanding. Saying to a teenager, "Don't stay out too late," leaves room for interpretation. It's better to say, "Be home by eleven o'clock." Improving the way you send verbal messages can eliminate potential conflicts.

What you say is weighed in light of your nonverbal communication—tone of voice, eye contact, posture, where attention is focused, following up words with action, and emotional pitch. All influence the messages your children receive. Saying, "I love you, too," without lowering the newspaper for a good-night kiss sends a message that makes the child question the sincerity of your love. Repeating threats again and again causes your word to lose its meaning. If you want your message to be clearly understood, make sure that the nonverbal clues agree with your words.

Listening

Listening can be difficult when trying to understand children who haven't fully developed their communication skills. It requires patience and focused effort. Beyond just listening to the words that you rely upon heavily with adults, you must learn to listen to the other cues used by children to communicate: their body language, facial expression, and emotional intensity.

In his book *Love Against Hate,* Dr. Karl Menninger said, "Listening is a magnetic and strange thing, a creative force. The friends who listen to us are the ones we move toward, and we want to sit in their radius. When we are listened to, it creates us, makes us unfold and expand." Listening is one of your best tools to help your children grow, especially during their teenage years when they are trying to discover their own approach to life. During the early years, children are hungry for instruction to show them how to live. Once they reach puberty, they desire a listening ear to help them test out their own theories of life. If you insist on lecturing instead of listening at this stage in their development, you may find that they gravitate away from you when you want to remain in touch enough to guide them safely to adulthood.

Giving and Receiving Feedback

Listening to children must be interactive, repeating what you thought they meant until what you are hearing agrees with what they are trying to say. As you try to communicate a message to your children, it's imperative that you make sure they understand by having them relay the message back to you. It's not enough to ask if they understand and have them say yes. They may think they understand when they really don't or say yes to try to please you. If you grow impatient with their inability to understand, you can cause them to close off instead of feeling free to keep asking for clarification until they really do understand.

The atmosphere that encourages good communication is one in which children feel safe to express themselves. If they are ridiculed, attacked verbally by name-calling and degrading remarks, or reprimanded for expressing their ideas and questions, they will learn that it isn't safe to openly communicate with you.

PERSONAL EVALUATION

- Are your verbal messages clearly communicated?
- How well do your verbal and nonverbal messages agree?

- Can you think of times when you sent double messages to your children? What effect did these double messages have on them?
- Do your family members ever complain that they don't think you are listening to them?
- Do you look your children in the eye whenever they speak to you?
- What is most difficult for you about attentively listening to your children? Distractions? Time? Disinterest?
- Do you give and receive feedback while communicating with your children to make sure the message received resembles the one sent?
- Can you think of times when your attitudes, actions, or messages created an atmosphere where your children didn't feel safe to express themselves openly?

ACTION

Today practice each phase of good communication skills with your children. Look them directly in the eye whenever you speak or listen to them. In your notebook, rate yourself on a scale of one to ten for each area (one is poor; ten is excellent): sending clear verbal messages, making sure nonverbal ones agree with verbal, listening, giving feedback, receiving feedback, and creating a positive atmosphere for communication. After each rating, list one practical thing you could do to improve in that area.

REFLECTION

What were the things you realized and felt as you practiced your communication skills? Do you believe that good communication is crucial for being able to build into the lives of your children? Do you think it's important to improve communication skills?

ENCOURAGEMENT

Every time you look your children in the eye or take the extra time to make sure you are hearing them, you are sending the nonverbal message that what they say really matters in this world.

FOOD FOR THOUGHT

People love to talk but hate to listen. Listening is not merely not talking, though even that is beyond most of our powers; it means taking a vigorous, human interest in what is being told us. You can listen like a blank wall or like a splendid auditorium where every sound comes back fuller and richer.
—Alice Duer Miller

Partnering with Your Children's Mother

Whether you are married or divorced, you need to partner with your children's mother as they are growing up. The old adage "Divide and conquer!" seems to come second nature to children. Any time they can get mom and dad on opposite sides of an issue, children think they are at an advantage. In reality, the more mother and father partner together in agreement while raising their children, the greater the benefit to the children. You will best serve your children by having a common understanding of what you are trying to accomplish as parents.

If you are married, the best thing you can do for your children is to model a healthy, loving relationship with your wife. Your children will learn how male-female relationships work by watching the interaction between their father and mother. In his book *The Best Dad Is a Good Lover*, Dr. Charlie Shedd said, "As I see it, my number one job as a father is to love my children's mother well." You will do your children a great service by devoting yourself to being a loving husband. You are not taking time away from your children when you take time to stay in love with your wife. Rather, the time you spend nurturing your relationship with your wife serves double duty as you provide a role model for your children to follow in shaping their view of a healthy marriage.

Dr. Shedd suggests two practical tips for keeping your marriage in good condition. The first is to have a weekly date; go out with your wife for the evening. The other is to spend at least fifteen minutes each day in heart-to-heart conversation with your wife regarding how each of you is doing on the inside.

Another thing you can do to partner with your wife is to set your goals in such a way that achieving them does not require you to control the behavior of everyone else in the home. Your fathering goals are for you. They should not be goals for ordering the lives of family members.

If you are divorced from your children's mother, you will need a closer-knit support group with whom to share your goals and from whom to receive help in covering your children's needs. When you consider the many needs of your children, you should determine whether these needs are being met in relationship with their mother. If not, you should identify persons who can help you do the things for your children that you can't do on your own.

You can gain valuable information about your children and their needs by listening to their mother's insights. The mother and the father bring unique perspectives to raising children. Whenever you are baffled by something about your children, consult their mother. She may have an understanding of the situation that can help you see it more clearly and be better able to deal with it from your perspective as their father.

Personal Evaluation

If You Are Married

- Have you shared your dreams, goals, and plans with your wife? If not, what keeps you from being able to do so?
- Have you expressed what you are trying to accomplish and identified the areas where you feel the need for extra support to keep you on track in terms of being a world-class father?
- Do you have a weekly date with your wife and a daily time of conversation pertaining to matters of the heart?

If You Are Divorced

- Have you identified the needs of your children that are being met by their mother?
- Have you identified persons to help cover the needs of your children that are not currently being met?
- Have you communicated these needs to the people involved and received commitments from them to give you and your children support?

Action

If you are married, set aside a specially designated time to discuss your 30-day journey with your wife. Consider how any changes you will be making affect your wife's schedule and the role she will play in your ongoing journey.

Clearly define your expectations of your children's

mother in terms of how the two of you will cooperate to meet the children's needs. If your expectations conflict with hers, negotiate expectations and commitments to best meet the needs of everyone involved, especially the children.

Double-check your support network of caregivers (those taking care of some of your children's needs). Are they cooperating with your overall goals for your children's well-being?

Make a commitment to establish a weekly date with your wife and a daily time of conversation. Start this week.

REFLECTION

How well do you partner with your children's mother to meet their needs?

ENCOURAGEMENT

Your willingness to cooperate with your children's mother is a vital part of being a world-class father.

FOOD FOR THOUGHT

The best combination of parents consists of a father who is gentle beneath his firmness, and a mother who is firm beneath her gentleness.
—Sydney J. Harris

Partnering with Other Caregivers

When ours was an agrarian society, a child was molded largely by the family. Families worked together, worshiped together, had common friends, listened to the same music, and had access to the same sources of information. Chances are good that the father personally had a relationship with all the people in a position to influence his children. That is not the case today.

In his book *Raising Positive Kids in a Negative World*, Zig Ziglar says, "You are what you are and where you are because of what has gone into your mind. You can change what you are and where you are by changing what goes into your mind." The truth of these statements has far-reaching implications for parents. Your children will be molded by what goes into their minds. To the degree you want to positively influence your children's growth and development, you must monitor what is going into their minds. Much of the input into your children's lives is coming from people you may not know personally, and you are less likely to know their philosophy of life.

Consider the sources from which your children are being mentally fed: teachers, baby-sitters, day-care workers, Sunday school teachers, television personalities, cartoon characters, musicians, music video performers, peers, parents of peers, youth workers, movie stars, and so on. Although you cannot control everything that goes into your children's minds, you can do some things to buffer these influences.

Know what is being taught in each child's classroom. You have the right to preview curriculum, meet your child's teacher, and discuss issues of concern about what is being taught. Teachers often welcome parental involvement in the classroom. If you have a flexible schedule, you may have the opportunity to volunteer an hour each week in the classroom and gain insight into exactly what your child is learning each day. Attend parent-teacher conferences, and communicate directly with the teacher any time you have questions or concerns.

Monitor the media input your children receive. Listen to the music and the lyrics; get to know the artists popular with your children's group of friends. Discuss the issues raised in the music. You may want to limit the music videos, television shows, and movies your children watch.

Get to know anyone who is taking on some aspect of care for your children. Monitor the time your children spend with them, what is going on during the time, what is being learned, and so on. Most parents need to rely on others outside their family to help with child care at times. According to Dr. Grace Ketterman, it is best if you can arrange for children to have one child-care provider rather than a host of caretakers who are not able to develop a deep, on-going relationship with the children.

PERSONAL EVALUATION

- How aware are you of what is going into your children's minds when they are not with you?
- How well do you know the people who provide child care when you are not able to care for your children directly?
- How well do you know each child's teacher and what is going on inside the child's classroom?
- How familiar are you with the content and phi-losophy being espoused in the entertainment your children are taking in?
- How well do you know your children's friends and their parents?

ACTION

Make a calendar that covers an entire week. For each day, fill in where your children typically spend their time. Looking over the calendar, draw out the following information:

- List all the people who directly care for your children and what you know about each one.
- List all the people your children spend time with regularly.
- What kind of information is being communi-cated to your children during these times?

- What media are they allowed to watch or listen to during the time spent there?
- What are the limits and values upheld in this environment?

From this exercise, list actions to take to get missing information. Make appointments with the people influencing your children so that you can get to know them and determine that what is going into your children's hearts and minds meets with your approval.

REFLECTION

Do you feel confident with the people who are providing care for your children? If not, what do you plan to do about it?

ENCOURAGEMENT

By taking the time to get to know the people who influence your children, you can protect your children and make sure they get the level of care they need.

FOOD FOR THOUGHT

Proverbs 4:23 asserts, "Keep your heart with all diligence, for out of it spring the issues of life." Until your children are old enough to guard their own hearts, it is up to you to protect them from negative influences.

Creating a Healthy Environment for Growing Up

According to Josiah G. Holland in *Gold Foil: Home*, "Home, in one form or another, is the great object of life." As a father, you have the power and privilege to create a home. With a little imagination and planning, your home can be the place your children and their friends gravitate toward. You may think the key to making your home a great place to be is to have all the latest gadgets and gizmos, the pool and the basketball court, the big screen TV and the latest video games. All of those amenities might be nice and certainly would attract the neighborhood children initially. However, those things do not cause children to feel at home and want to stay.

Children are drawn by laughter; they stay for love. Children and youths today hunger for a place where they are known and loved; a place where they are not an interruption to something "important"; a place where they don't get the message that they are in the way. Your home can be designed to become the place in your neighborhood where your children and their friends want to be whenever they have the choice.

What are the elements of a healthy environment for growing children? It will be a place designed for fun, where games are played, where children are welcome to make an occasional mess as long as they clean it up, where laughter and surprises are the common fare. It will be a place that has clearly defined rules, which are respectfully enforced. Children will know what to expect and what is expected of them. They will know what areas are open to them and what areas are off limits, what's O.K. to touch and what's not.

It will be a place designed for learning. Your children will have a special place and the tools they need to study and learn. Books will be available and story times frequent. Creative ventures will be encouraged and assisted.

It will be a place where forgiveness is commonly practiced by all, where mistakes are not ridiculed but are consistently corrected. It will be a place where children can find open arms after they have had a difficult day and ears ready to listen when they want to talk out a problem.

It will be a place where there are nourishment and refreshments for growing bodies, minds, and spirits. It will be a place where the people know them, are proud of them, believe in them, support them, encourage them, and give them the backing to make it in life. It will be a place where their victories will always be recognized and celebrated and their defeats cushioned. It will be a place where they can always find a warm hug.

PERSONAL EVALUATION

- Have you ever taken time to use your imagination to dream up the kind of environment you are trying to create for your children?

- Is your home a place where you enjoy spending time?
- Is your home a place where your children and their friends want to spend time? Why or why not?

ACTION

Rate your home on a scale of one to ten on the following (one is poor; ten is excellent):

- Our home is a fun place to be.
- Our home is filled with laughter and surprises.
- Our home is comfortable and inviting.
- Our home has reasonable rules, respectfully enforced.
- Our home has ready nourishment for growing minds.
- Our home has ready nourishment for growing bodies.
- Our home has ready nourishment for growing spirits.
- Our home is a place where learning and reading are encouraged.
- Our home is a place where creative endeavors are encouraged.
- Our home is a place where forgiveness is commonly practiced.
- Our home is a place where victories are celebrated and defeats cushioned.
- Our home is a place where a child can find open arms and ears.

- Our home is a place where children are not an imposition.
- Our home is a place where hugs are offered frequently.
- Our home is a place where guests are welcomed.
- Our home is a place where we're proud of our children and their friends.

Review your ratings, and decide what you would like to do to make your home environment more inviting.

REFLECTION

What would it take to transform your home into a healthy environment for growing up? Is this something you consider to be worthy of your efforts?

ENCOURAGEMENT

When you make your home a more enjoyable place for your children, you are doing them and yourself a favor.

FOOD FOR THOUGHT

A loving home can be a child's first glimpse of heaven.

The Power of Your Praise

There would be little argument that Ted Turner and Henry Fonda represent undisputed successes in their respective fields of business and acting. Millions of people around the globe would agree with this statement without much thought. However, when it comes to their own estimation of what it meant to be a success, they both looked to their fathers for the final word.

In the book *Father: The Figure and the Force*, Christopher P. Andersen tells the story of how media mogul Ted Turner's father, a successful businessman, committed suicide at age 53. He quoted Ted Turner as saying, "My father died when I was 24. That left me alone because I had counted on him to make the judgement of whether or not I was a success."

Andersen relates what Henry Fonda called his "most important memory":

> Fonda's father, a solid Midwesterner, viewed his son's interest in acting with disdain. . . . Fonda senior grudgingly went along with the rest of the family to watch his son's first performance on stage, and when Henry came home he found his father glowering behind the newspaper while his mother and sister were involved in a heated discussion about flaws in the production. Finally a voice erupted from behind the newspaper. "Shut up," commanded Hank's father. "He was perfect."

"It is touching," Andersen says, "that in telling that story, Fonda seemed to be confiding that this was the one true moment of candor between father and son."

Never underestimate the power of your praise. It has tremendous power to build your children up and give them the confidence they need to succeed in life. Your words of criticism have the power to destroy, perhaps much more than you realize. Psychologists have found that as many as nine positive comments are needed to counteract the effect of one criticism.

On the other hand, children respond readily to those who affirm them. "Mister Rogers" is the longest-running children's program on public television. It has won virtually every award in its field. Why is Mr. Rogers so irresistible to children (and even some teens and adults who secretly watch his program)? The answer can probably be summed up in a few words: *respect, acceptance,* and *affirmation.*

If you want to turn to someone who will look you in the eye, validate your feelings, accept you as you are, and still affirm you, you can always depend on Mr. Rogers! And millions of children do each day. How much more powerful it is when respect, acceptance, and affirmation come from the child's father.

You have the power and the opportunity to let your children experience the unconditional love and affirmation they long for. Even if they don't always behave as you want them to behave, you can affirm them and find something worthy of praise. If you look only to discover and point out the mistakes, your children will see themselves as failures. If you look to find the good and praise it, your children will begin to see themselves as worthwhile and capable people.

PERSONAL EVALUATION

- Do you accept your children and love them unconditionally?
- How often do you praise your children (for their talents, accomplishments, efforts, appearance, and so on)?
- What is the ratio of praise to criticism that you give your children?
- When have you seen a positive response after giving your children genuine praise?

ACTION

In your fathering notebook, make a list for each child of everything you can find to praise. Without being artificial, make a point of looking your children in the eye and giving them genuine praise. Write down the response and effect you see the power of your praise having in their lives.

REFLECTION

Think back on a specific instance when you received praise from your father. What effect has your father's praise (or lack of praise) had on your life?

ENCOURAGEMENT

Every man wants to be effective in his children's lives. By using the power of praise, you are making positive contributions to their lives on a daily basis.

FOOD FOR THOUGHT

A father's blessing cannot be drowned in water nor consumed by fire.

—Russian Proverb

Reevaluate and Give Yourself Credit

On Day 10 of your journey, you selected a few specific goals in each of the three facets of fathering. Now is the time to reconsider the goals you chose and see if you have reached the objectives you set before you. You also made a form on Day 16 to examine the investments you were making in your children's lives. Look over what you have learned from these exercises and decide what changes are necessary. If you didn't reach your original goals, set a new target date for completion.

Although you have reached the end of the 30-day journey outlined in this book, your personal journey continues. My hope is that you have come to recognize that you are all the father your children need. You have the love, the assets, the power, and the understanding to be everything they need in a father. Sure, you have some areas that demand continued attention, but every human relationship requires ongoing care.

We have defined being a world-class father to mean balancing your resources and abilities in each of three areas: fulfilling your role and responsibilities, developing loving relationships, and bringing out the best in them as you launch them into life. As you continue to keep this healthy balance, you will grow as a world-class father, and your confidence in the realm of fathering will grow as well.

PERSONAL EVALUATION

You may tend to underestimate the value of what you have done during this journey. You deserve to be commended for the time, consideration, effort, and self-evaluation you have devoted to this journey. Give yourself credit for what you have done. Discuss your journey with others. Do something to celebrate the completion of your journey. Perhaps you may want to have a family celebration so that all members of your family are allowed to share how your completion of the action steps in this book has affected their lives and their relationship with you.

You have already taken decisive action to learn about and consider each facet of fathering. You have compiled your notebook with goal sheets and forms to follow toward achieving your worthy goals. Why stop now? Each time you achieve a goal in each area, choose another to replace it. In this way you will continue to grow and find a sense of confidence that comes from knowing you are moving continually in the right direction.

The important thing is not to lose momentum. Each day, one day at a time, keep your dreams clearly in sight, your goals well defined, your tasks identified, your obstacles targeted for attack, and your relationship growing. The journey continues.

ACTION

Plan to continue using your fathering personal growth notebook to record and monitor your progress toward family-related goals.

Review all that you have learned in the course of the last thirty days and the discoveries you have made. List the things you have learned about yourself and your family as a result of taking this journey.

List the life changes you have made as a result of taking this journey.

List the areas of interest you have discovered to be explored later. Include a list of books, tapes, and other resources you plan to explore.

Hold a family meeting to discuss your experiences and discoveries during your 30-day journey.

Once more, write detailed descriptions of what you know of each child's body, mind, and spirit.

REFLECTION

How do you feel about yourself as a father now that you have completed this journey? After taking your journey, do you have a sense of balance in all three areas? Are you taking clearly defined steps and making commitments to achieve balance in all three areas? Are you beginning to confidently see yourself as a world-class father? Open the envelopes holding the descriptions of your children written on Day 1 and Day 9. Consider how your understanding of each unique child has grown during your 30-day journey.

ENCOURAGEMENT

You are among the ranks of those fathers who have demonstrated that they truly are willing to go the distance to become world-class.

FOOD FOR THOUGHT

If you observe a really happy man, you will find him building a boat, writing a symphony, educating his son, growing double dahlias in his garden, or looking for dinosaur eggs in the Gobi desert. He will not be searching for happiness as if it were a collar button that has rolled under the radiator. He will not be striving for it as a goal in itself. He will have become aware that he is happy in the course of living life 24 crowded hours of the day.

—W. Beran Wolfe

Sometimes problems are too difficult to handle alone on a 30-day journey. If you feel that you need additional help, please talk with one of the counselors at New Life Treatment Centers. The call is confidential and free.

1-800-277-LIFE